WHO IS OUR EXAMPLE?

Third Grade Workbook

Michelle Richardson

Camille Kohner

Educational and Theological Advisors

Rev. Richard M. Hogan

Rev. John M. LeVoir

Mary Jo Smith

IMAGE OF GOD SERIES

IMAGE OF GOD, INC., BROOKLYN CENTER, MN
IGNATIUS PRESS, SAN FRANCISCO, CA

Nihil obstat: Mark B. Dosh
                Censor Librorum

Imprimatur: ✠ John R. Roach, D.D.
                Archbishop of St. Paul and Minneapolis
                July 25, 1989

Cover design and illustrations: Barbara Harasyn

For additional information about
the Image of God program: 1-800-635-3827

Published 1991 by Ignatius Press, San Franciso
© 1989 Image of God, Inc.
All rights reserved
ISBN 0-89870-330-1
Printed in Hong Kong
Third Edition

TABLE OF CONTENTS

LETTER TO PARENTS

Dear Parents,

This year your child will be using the "Who Is Our Example?" third grade program from the Image of God series. This series is centered on a new subjective emphasis found in the writings and teachings of Pope John Paul II. This subjective turn stresses the dignity of each individual as a person made in the image of God.

The third grade program has as its focus two key ideas: Christ and the Church. These key ideas form the unifying element of the lessons. The material in each lesson revolves around fundamentals of our Faith stated in terms the children can understand and remember.

You, as parents, are the primary religious educators of your children. The "Who Is Our Example?" program has many materials that are sent home to provide a basis for parent-child faith discussions. There are textbook pages for every lesson. Sometimes your child will bring home a completed activity to share. Sometimes, though, it will be up to you, as parents, to complete the activity with your child.

It is hoped that through this program you and your child will grow in faith together.

Unit 1

The Mystery of God

1 The Mystery of God

WORDS TO KNOW

mystery: A truth that our minds cannot completely understand.

being: Someone that is, that exists.

choose: To decide; to make a choice.

believe: To know and to accept by faith.

source: A person, place, or thing from which something comes.

robed: Clothed with a robe.

image: A copy or reflection of something.

perfection: Without mistake; excellence; completeness.

beauty: A quality that is delightful to look at, to listen to, or to think about.

truth: Something true or right.

love: To choose freely to give oneself to God and others.

reveal: To make known; to show.

inspire: To give someone an idea to act.

Bible: The book that contains God's word.

What might God look like?

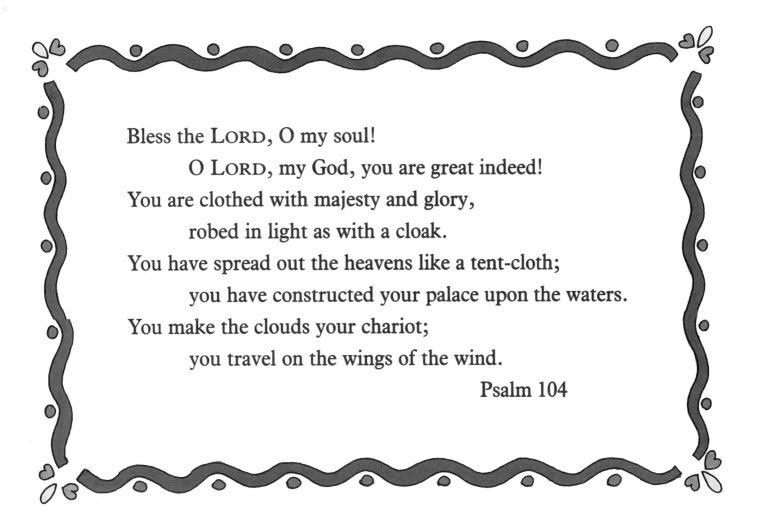

Bless the LORD, O my soul!

      O LORD, my God, you are great indeed!

You are clothed with majesty and glory,

      robed in light as with a cloak.

You have spread out the heavens like a tent-cloth;

      you have constructed your palace upon the waters.

You make the clouds your chariot;

      you travel on the wings of the wind.

                        Psalm 104

When we are asked, "What might God look like?", we may think of Him as our Creator robed in glory above the clouds—just like the one in the picture! We cannot see God.

Still, we can imagine what He might look like.

Then, who is God? God is the source of all life. He is the all-powerful, all-wise, and all-loving Being Who created everything. He is a mystery that we cannot completely understand.

Because God is a supreme mystery, how do we come to know Him? We can come to know God by studying the things He has made, by reading Bible stories about Him, and by listening to what the Church teaches.

All of creation was wonderfully planned and was created by God from nothing. The earth on which we live spins on its own axis. Day turns into night, and night turns into day. The seasons return year after year at the same time, providing sunshine and showers for all of God's creatures. Plans such as these show us that God is all-wise. The handiwork of creation shows us that He is all-powerful.

Above all the fine things God has made, He created living persons. When God creates, He gives. He who gives something to others loves. This wise and powerful God must have loved us very much because He gave us so much. Creation shows us that God is all-loving.

From the tiny ant to the lion, all creatures have a purpose. Their habits, powers, beauty, and perfection remind us of how mysterious life is. Only a living God could create such living beings for us!

God is the all-powerful, all-wise, and all-loving Being Who created everything. He is the source of everything. In addition, there was nothing before God. He was not created. God always was, He is now, and He always will be.

How wonderful
are your works,
O Lord!
You have made
all things
from nothing.

We know that
you are wise
and powerful!
Thank you
for your
marvelous gifts!

We learned that we can come to know God by studying the wonders of His world. But God also reveals Himself to us by speaking to us. His word can be found in stories about Him in the Bible.

Long ago, before there were any books, God spoke to a certain group of people. He revealed His great power in the things He did for them. They were so inspired by His words and deeds that they told stories about Him.

Years passed and other people began writing down those stories about the wonder of our Creator. The writings were saved and collected over many hundreds of years. A book was formed by the Church. One of the ways God speaks to us today is through this book. It tells us about God. This book of holy writings is called "the Bible".

The word *Bible* comes from the Greek word *biblion*, meaning "book". The Bible is not just one book; it is a library of books in one volume. The Bible is one of the ways that the Church teaches us about God. There are other things about God that are not in the Bible. The Church teaches us these things, too. In order for us to know all there is to know about God, we should listen to the teachings of the Church.

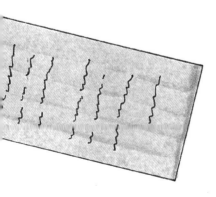

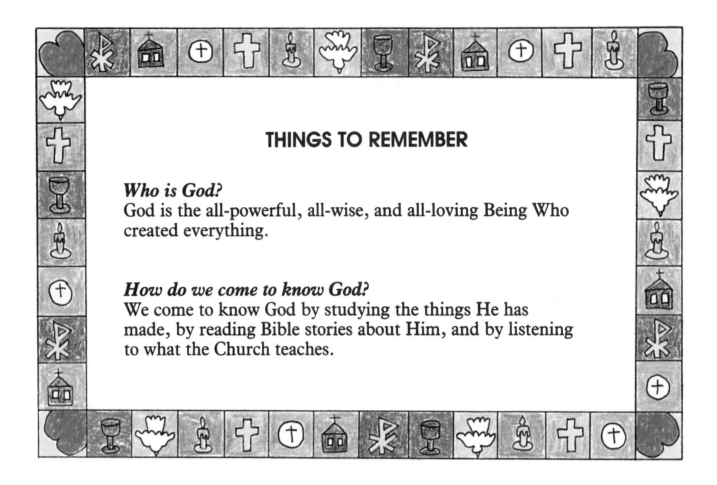

THINGS TO REMEMBER

Who is God?
God is the all-powerful, all-wise, and all-loving Being Who created everything.

How do we come to know God?
We come to know God by studying the things He has made, by reading Bible stories about Him, and by listening to what the Church teaches.

Cut out the words. Match them to the definitions on the next page. Glue the words and definitions together on a separate sheet of paper.

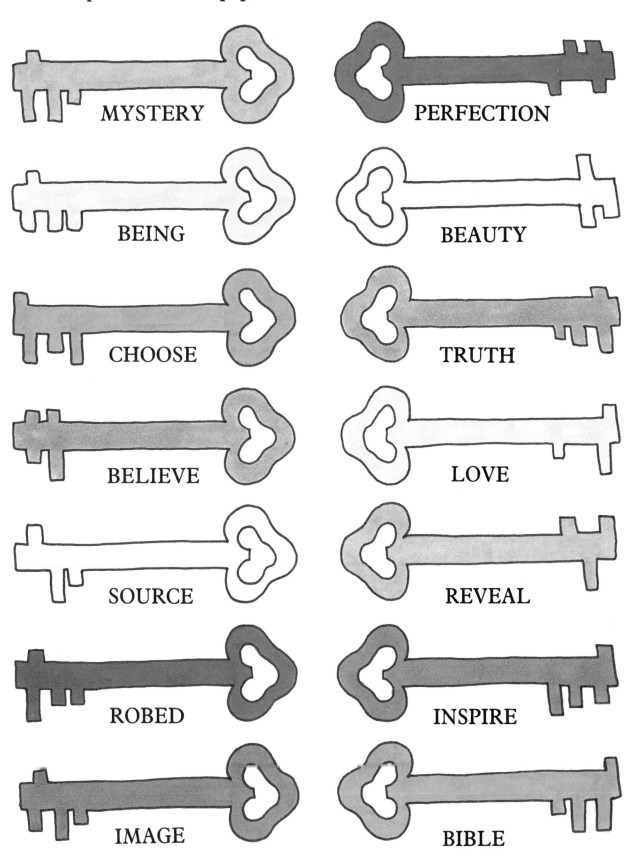

MYSTERY

PERFECTION

BEING

BEAUTY

CHOOSE

TRUTH

BELIEVE

LOVE

SOURCE

REVEAL

ROBED

INSPIRE

IMAGE

BIBLE

Cut out the definitions. Match them with the words on the previous page. Glue the words and definitions together on a separate sheet of paper.

 a truth that our minds cannot completely understand

 someone that is, that exists

 the book that contains God's word

 to make known; to show

 something true or right

 a person, place, or thing from which something comes

 to know and to accept by faith

 to choose freely to give oneself to God and others

 a copy or reflection of something

 without mistake; excellence; completeness

 to give someone an idea to act

 clothed with a robe

 a quality that is delightful to look at, listen to, or think about

 to decide; to make a choice

2 Three Persons in One God

WORDS TO KNOW

person: Someone who has a mind and a will.

There is only one God. Yet there are three Persons in God. God the Father, God the Son, and God the Holy Spirit are three Persons in one God. We call the mystery of three Persons in one God the Blessed Trinity.

We can *think* of God the Father as our Creator; we can *think* of God the Son as our Teacher and Savior; and we can *think* of God the Holy Spirit as our Helper. We only *think* of them as acting separately, but God the Father, Son, and Holy Spirit create, teach, save, and help together.

Remember, the Blessed Trinity is a mystery. It is difficult for us to understand. To help us learn about each Person, we are going to look at each one in succession.

God the Father's perfect image, God the Son, became man. We call Him Jesus. Through His teaching, Jesus tells us that we are images of God. He also teaches us how we should act as images of God. As our Savior, Jesus returned God's love and helps us return God's love.

God the Holy Spirit comes to us to give us grace, God's life. He comes to us every time we receive the sacraments. He helps us act as images of God.

Again, we must remember that God (all three Persons) creates us, saves and teaches us, helps us, and loves us. All three Persons work together as one.

When God the Father created the world and all of us, He showed us His power. He brought the world into existence out of nothing. He also created us in His image and likeness.

In the beginning, before God created the heavens and the earth, there was darkness everywhere. Then God said, "Let there be light", and there was light. He called the light "day" and the darkness "night".

Next, God made the blue sky. He made the beautiful oceans, lakes, rivers, and streams. He filled the sky with everything that flies and the waters with everything that swims.

Between the waters He placed dry lands, grassy fields, hills, and mountains. To add to the landscape, God created flowers and trees. He then made every kind of animal: wild and tame, big and small.

God looked at everything that He had made. He was pleased.

Then God made Adam, the first man. Adam was special. He was an image of God. He could share God's life. He could think, love, and work. Adam was a person.

Even though Adam enjoyed taking care of God's world, he was lonesome. He was the only person with a body! There were angels. Angels are persons, but they do not have bodies. Adam could not see them and talk to them. He wanted to share his life with someone.

God did not want Adam to be lonely. So God created the first woman—Eve. Although Eve did not look exactly like Adam, she was created in the image and likeness of God, too. Adam and Eve loved each other as God's images. They formed the first family.

God told Adam and Eve that He had made the world and everything in it for them. He asked them to take care of everything in this world.
    —Adapted from Genesis 1:1–31

We can think of God the Father as our Creator. However, we must remember that God (all three Persons) created us. All three Persons work together as one.

LIVING THE LESSON

1. Who created the world and everything in it out of nothing?

   _____

2. Whom can we think of as our Creator?

   _____

3. In the beginning, there was darkness everywhere. Then God said:

   _____

   _____

4. Next, God created the sky and the water. What forms of life can be found in the sky and water?

   _____

   _____

5. What forms of life can be found on land?

   _____

   _____

6. The first man, Adam, was special. Why?

   _____

   _____

7. The first woman, Eve, was special. Why?

   _____

   _____

8. Adam and Eve loved each other as God's images. They formed the first

   _____

Fill in the blanks with letters to form words that we can use to describe God the Father.

C _ _ _ _ _ _

_ _ _ _ _ _ R

_ _ _ E _ _ _ _

A _ _ _ _ _ _ _

_ _ _ _ _ _ _ T

_ O _ _ _ _

R _ _ _ _ _ _

Words to choose from:

Powerful   **Almighty**   **Creator**   **Perfect**

Loving   **Reveals**   **Father**

An identical image of God the Father does exist. He is the second Person of the Blessed Trinity, God the Son.

When Jesus was a baby, some of the people of that time knew that He had come to teach them the truth and to save them from sin! Read the following story about two of those people.

The Presentation in the Temple

After the birth of the baby Jesus, Mary and Joseph took Him to Jerusalem to present Him to the Lord. There was a man in Jerusalem by the name of Simeon. Simeon was a kind and loving man. He was old. Simeon was very holy. The Holy Spirit was with him.

When Mary and Joseph arrived at the temple, Simeon was already there. When he saw Mary and Joseph carrying baby Jesus, Simeon went up to them. He took the baby Jesus in his arms and prayed out loud saying, "Now, Master, I can die peacefully, for I have seen the glory of the Lord."

Mary and Joseph were amazed at what Simeon had to say about Jesus. Simeon told them that their child would speak the truth about who we are and how we should act. He told them that many people would not accept what Jesus would say. But he also said that many people would believe in what Jesus would say.

Anna, an eighty-four-year-old widow, was also in the temple. She saw baby Jesus too. She gave thanks to God the Father for allowing her to see Jesus. Then she went to tell all of the people who were waiting for news that the Savior had come!
—Adapted from Luke 2:22–38

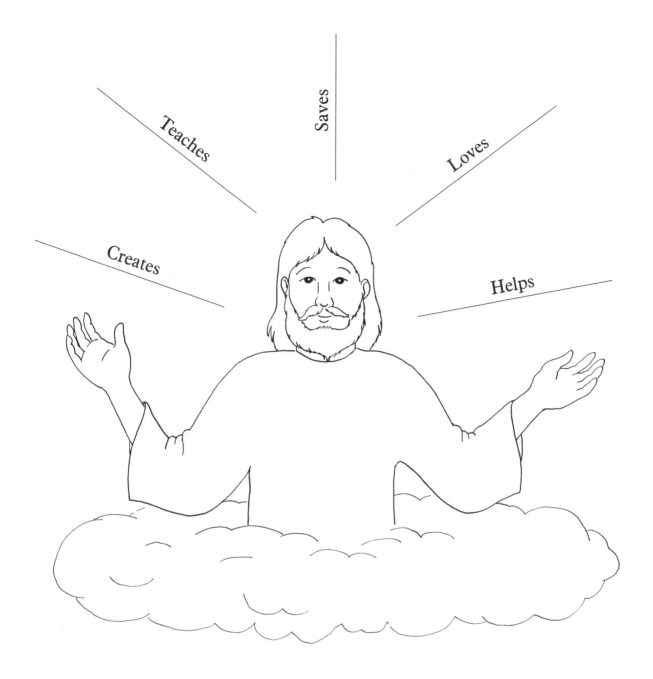

God the Son is the perfect image of God the Father. He became man to be our Teacher and Savior. Through His teaching, Jesus tells us that we are images of God. He also teaches us how we should act as images of God.

When Jesus, God the Son, died on the cross, He freed us from sin and returned the Father's love. He also made it possible for us to return the Father's love.

We can think of God the Son as our Teacher and Savior. However, we must remember that God (all three Persons) creates us, saves us, helps us, and teaches us. All three Persons work together as one.

Fill in the blanks with letters that form words we can use to describe God the Son.

S _ _ _ _ _ _

_ _ A _ _

_ _ V _ _ _

_ I _ _

_ O _ _

R _ _ _ _ _ _ _

Words to choose from:

Savior　　　　**Life**　　　　**Lord**

Redeemer　　　**Shepherd**　　**Image**

The Apostles were gathered together, all in one place. Suddenly, a noise like a strong wind filled the entire house that they were in. Tongues of fire appeared above each one of them. They were all filled with the Holy Spirit.

The noise caused a large crowd to gather. Everyone in the crowd was from a different country. When the Apostles were speaking, they all spoke a different language. Yet every one of the people could understand what the Apostles were saying.

All of the people in the crowd were amazed! They asked one another, "Aren't these people Galilean? Then how does each of us hear them in his own language?"

Peter stood up, raised his voice, and said, "Listen to my words. God promised King David that He would send us a Savior. God also promised that He would never leave us.

"The Savior Jesus did come. And, as you have just seen, Jesus sent us the Holy Spirit to be with us always. He will care for us and never leave us. Repent and be baptized, every one of you, in the name of Jesus Christ for the forgiveness of your sins; and you will receive the gift of the Holy Spirit."
—Adapted from Acts 2:1–12, 30–40

When the crowd gathered at the coming of the Holy Spirit, all of the people could understand the Apostles. This was a sign that the Holy Spirit wanted all people to know that He is there to help them with His grace.

When the Holy Spirit comes to give us grace, He will not come to us in tongues of fire. He will, however, help us act as brighter images of God.

We can think of God the Holy Spirit as our Helper. However, we must remember that God (all three Persons) creates us, saves and teaches us, and helps us. All three Persons work together as one.

ACROSS

1. The second Person of the Blessed Trinity is God the _____.
2. Jesus is our _____.
3 and 4. God the Holy Spirit _____ us to _____ as images of God.
5. God the Holy Spirit is our _____.
6. The Holy Spirit brings God's life called _____.
7. Jesus is the _____ image of God the Father.
8. God is very _____.
9 and 12. The Blessed Trinity is _____ _____ in one God.
10. The three Persons _____ and work as one.
11. Each of us is an _____ of God.

DOWN

1 and 2. Jesus _____ us from _____.
 7. The Holy Spirit first came to the Apostles during _____.
13. God created the world out of _____.
14. God the Father is our _____.
15. God is _____.
16. The first Person of the Blessed Trinity is God the _____.
17. The third Person of the Blessed Trinity is God the _____ Spirit.

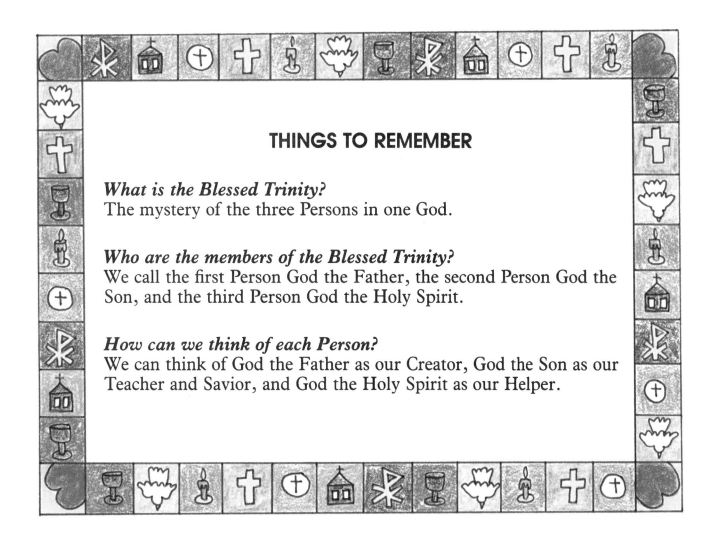

THINGS TO REMEMBER

What is the Blessed Trinity?
The mystery of the three Persons in one God.

Who are the members of the Blessed Trinity?
We call the first Person God the Father, the second Person God the Son, and the third Person God the Holy Spirit.

How can we think of each Person?
We can think of God the Father as our Creator, God the Son as our Teacher and Savior, and God the Holy Spirit as our Helper.

Fill in the blanks with letters that form words that we can use to describe the Holy Spirit.

H _ _ _ _

_ **O** _ _ _

_ **L** _ _ _

_ _ _ **Y**

_ _ _ _ _ _ _ _ _ _ **S**

_ **P** _ _ _ _ _

_ **I** _ _ _ _

_ **R** _ _ _

_ _ **I** _ _ _

_ _ _ _ _ _ _ _ _ **T**

Words to choose from:

Life	Guides	Sacraments
Holy	Loves	Pentecost
Spirit	Grace	Giving
	Helps	

28

3 Persons Loving As God Loves

Loving as God Loves within Families

Each of the three divine Persons of the Blessed Trinity gives Himself totally to the others. Because the three Persons perfectly love one another, they form a kind of family.

As images of God, we are called to love as God loves. When we love others, we form a kind of family with them.

A kind of family is formed when two or more persons work together, love each other, and help each other love as God loves. There are three kinds of families that we are studying. The first kind of family *is* the family! A family begins when a man and a woman marry. They promise to love each other, work together, and help each other love as God loves.

The second kind of family is the group of persons in the work place. Our work place is school. This kind of family is formed when students and teachers work together, love each other, and help each other love as God loves.

Finally, the sacrament of Baptism joins us to another family—God's family. The people within the Church work together, love each other, and help each other love as God loves.

THE BIRTHDAY PARTY

Tommy's birthday is this Saturday. He is very excited! His family plans to have a party for him. Everyone is invited—grandparents, aunts and uncles, and friends from school.

To have a successful party, everyone in the family must work together. This calls for a family meeting. Tommy's mother decided to have the meeting Friday after supper.

Read the following play to find out what happened.

Cast of Characters

Narrator

John Martin, age 17

Sarah Martin, age 13

Tommy Martin, age 9

Mr. Martin (Dad)

Grandma

Grandpa

Mrs. Martin (Mom)

30

Narrator: It's Friday night. The Martin family is gathered around the kitchen table after supper. All of the dishes have been cleared and washed. Mrs. Martin has a pencil, a list of jobs, and a grocery list.

Mom: We all know that tomorrow is a special day for Tommy. We want to do our best to make it fun for everyone. First, the house needs to be cleaned. I need a volunteer to scrub the floors.

Sarah: I'll do it. I've had a lot of practice. And, when I'm finished, I'll even do the vacuuming!

Dad: Yardwork is my specialty! I'll take care of that. We'll need a lot of food. John, why don't you do the shopping? Mom will give you the list.

John: No problem, Dad! I'll need the car keys.

Dad: Okay, but remember, go to the store and back, with no *additional* passengers!

Mom: I'll give you the list tomorrow morning, John. All of you, remember to clean your bedrooms! Tommy, Grandma and Grandpa will be staying in your room tomorrow. You'll be sleeping in John's room. Sarah, Aunt Terry and Uncle Ed will be staying downstairs. Please make sure the sheets, blankets, and pillows are ready for them. I will look over all rooms after lunch on Saturday. Are there any questions?

Family: No!

Narrator: It is now Saturday morning. Everyone begins to prepare for the party.

Mom: Let's get going on our chores, everyone! John, please take Tommy to the store with you.

Narrator: After Tommy and John have left, Mom, Dad, and Sarah pull out the decorations from behind the sofa.

31

Mom: We need to get these up before Tommy gets home, so we don't have much time! Dad, you take care of the back yard. Sarah, you take care of the kitchen, and I'll decorate the living room.

Narrator: By lunch time the house was ready. Everyone gathered around the kitchen table.

Mom: Our love for each other was easy to see. Everyone chipped in and helped. No one complained. I guess that's what it means to be members of a family! We all work together, love each other, and help each other love as God loves. I'm so proud of all of you!

Narrator: It's time for the party! The doorbell rings. Sarah answers it.

Grandma: The house looks wonderful, Sarah! How did the family do it all?

Sarah: Everyone in the family helped out. Mom says that we are all members of the family. We work together, love each other, and help each other love as God loves.

Grandma: I agree with your mom.

Grandpa: Now, where is that birthday boy?

Sarah: He's in the kitchen. Go ahead and join him! Mom, Dad, and John are in there, too.

Narrator: The birthday party was a big success! Dad visited with everyone and didn't burn the hamburgers. John didn't tease Tommy at all. Everyone helped Mom with the food. Sarah washed the dishes without being asked, and Tommy was thankful for every gift he received. The Martins showed us what a family should be—a group of persons who work together, love each other, and help each other love as God loves.

When members of a family work together and help each other, they are imitating God. They are loving as God loves.

THE SCHOOL'S FAMILY

Our class is like a large family. We need to work together, love each other, and help each other love as God loves. In the classroom we all need to work together so we are all able to learn. Classroom rules help us do this. Can you name some classroom rules?

1. _____

_____

_____

2. _____

_____

_____

3. _____

_____

_____

4. _____

_____

_____

Sometimes you may not feel very important, but what you have to offer the class is important. Each one of us is working hard to make our school the best learning place that it can be. When we work together, we form a kind of family in the school. We work together, love each other, and help each other love as God loves.

God's Family, the Church

The sacrament of Baptism joins all of us in one family—God's family, the Church. As members of this family, we should work together, love each other, and help each other love as God loves.

There are many ways in which people work together in God's family. Can you think of some of the ways people help out in your church? Many people help out at Mass. Some people are Eucharistic ministers, readers, ushers, altar servers, or choir members. Some people help in other ways, too. Some teach religion classes, and some collect food or clothing to give to the poor.

When you give your time and talents to others, you are showing your love for them. All of the people who are baptized form the family of the Church. They should all work together, love each other, and help each other love as God loves.

THINGS TO REMEMBER

What is our calling in life?
To love as God loves.

How do we love as God loves?
By forming groups of persons who work together, love each other, and help each other love as God loves.

My Baptism

My full name

_____

My parents

_____

My godparents

_____

_____

The date and time of my baptism

_____

The church where I was baptized

_____

The priest who baptized me

_____

Unit 2

Who

We Are:

Images of God

4 Who Are We?

WORDS TO KNOW

ability: Being able to act.
decide: To choose.
think: To have in mind; to form an idea in the mind.
understand: To know the meaning of.

image: A copy or reflection of something.
likeness: Similarity; having something in common.
dominion: To be in charge of.
creature: Something or someone made from nothing by God.

Who Are We?

Two students, Tim and Joan, came to their new school for their first day of class. Both of them had to find the gym, but neither one knew where it was.

Tim said, "I think we should look for the office first. If we ask the secretaries, they will show us how to get to the gym."

But Joan said, "I think we should stop at the nearest classroom and ask. Looking for the office will take too much time."

Tim said, "Look. Since we each think our idea is the best, why don't you try your way and I'll try mine. I'll meet you in the gym."

"Okay," said Joan, "I'll see you there."

Tim and Joan could think about what to do and could choose what action to take. Like Tim and Joan, we are images of God. We are persons. We can think and choose. We can think and choose to act as images of God.

ACTIVITY: Cut out the words on page 43 and place them in the proper boxes. Watch out! Some of the boxes will remain blank.

Animals

People

People and Animals

HUNT	THINK	CHOOSE
EAT	SLEEP	LOVE
DRINK	PAINT	CLIMB
LAUGH	RUN	SING
DRIVE	SWIM	KNIT
COLOR	READ	SCREAM

43

God created the world and everything in it.

God created the world and everything in it. God made all kinds of wild animals and creeping things. Then God made man and woman in His image and likeness.

God said, "Let them have dominion over the fish of the sea, the birds of the air, and the cattle, and over all the wild animals and all the creatures that crawl on the ground."

—Genesis 1:24–26

Animals cannot think or freely choose. They can only live their lives looking for food and protection for themselves. They do not determine what to do or not to do in the same way we do.

Of all the living things God created on earth, only we are made in His image and likeness. God thinks and chooses. As images of God, we can think and choose. We can think about how we should act. We can choose to love or not to love. When we think and choose to love as God loves, we act as His images. If we are not thinking and choosing to love as God does, we can change and begin to think and choose as images of God.

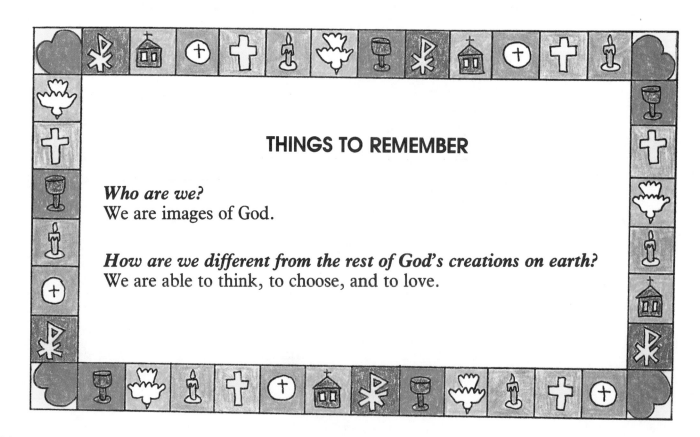

THINGS TO REMEMBER

Who are we?
We are images of God.

How are we different from the rest of God's creations on earth?
We are able to think, to choose, and to love.

5 God Gives Us the Power to Think

WORDS TO KNOW

mind: What we think with; where our knowledge is stored.

think: To use one's mind.

store: To keep.

parable: A short story that teaches a religious lesson.

Pharisees: A group who kept all the rules and tried to make other people keep the rules. They were more often concerned with keeping the rules than with loving God.

synagogue: A building where Jewish people pray.

servants: Helpers in the house.

in charge: Be responsible for something.

Our world is filled with so many fascinating things. Every day we seem to learn something new. In reading we learn new words. With those new words we can read about people we have never met and places we have never seen.

Dogs go to obedience school. But, unlike all of us, they do not use books. Dogs cannot think as we do. Their owners practice with the dogs all of the things the teachers have trained the dogs to do.

$m = 10^{-9}$ gms

Hmmmm... $m = \dfrac{E}{c^2}$

God has given us minds to think and to store the special information that we want to keep.

Our minds can be compared to a bedroom closet. At first the closet seems so big. You begin to collect things to fill it. You put so many of your favorite things inside your closet that it becomes overloaded. The closet cannot handle any more, and everything falls out when you open it.

When your closet is cluttered, finding a favorite object becomes very difficult. You dig through all the things you do not need, searching. You throw everything else out of the closet until you've found what you are looking for. You're overjoyed, until you see the pile of objects that need to be placed back into the closet. Oh no, cleaning time!

Carefully, you check through all of the things on the floor and the things left in the closet. You ask yourself, "Which ones do I want to keep? Which ones are not needed anymore?"

After separating your objects into two piles, you begin to place the things you want to keep back into the closet, neatly. What a change! The closet looks great! Things are much easier to find now.

Like our bedroom closet, our minds can become cluttered, too. We continue to learn new things. We need to clear our minds of the things that should not be there and remember only the things that we need to know.

New information comes to us every day. In the morning, when we want to eat breakfast, we look for our favorite cereal. But when we open the cupboard, we see that Mom bought something new. So we decide to give the new cereal a try. We remember how our favorite brand tastes. We find that we still like our favorite brand the best.

At school, during math class, we learn that $2 + 2 + 2 = 6$. But our teacher tells us that $2 \times 3 = 6$, also. So we decide to use 2×3 instead of $2 + 2 + 2$, because multiplying is quicker.

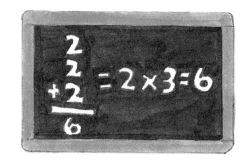

At home, your little sister is in your room again, making a mess of your model airplanes. You've yelled at her before, but there she is again. You know that yelling is not the way to keep your sister away from your models. You think about how much she likes the models, so you have the idea to make her a model of her own. Maybe that will keep her out of your room.

We keep all these new experiences in our minds and remember them.

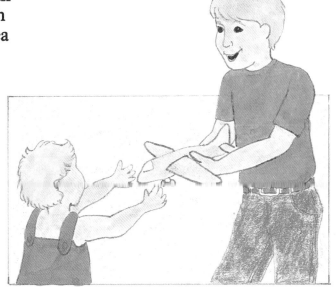

Mind Closet

_____ _____

_____ _____

_____ _____

_____ _____

_____ _____

Read the following list of information. From your experiences, think of the things you should keep in your "mind closet". Cut out the items that you should keep and glue them neatly in your "closet" on page 52.

Knowledge of God

Unkind words

Birthdays and holidays

The Ten Commandments

Hobbies

Dangerous things

A friend's mistake

Names of friends

Prayers

Ways to get out of doing work

Special places you have visited

Favorite sports

Ways to tease someone

School subjects

The Parable of the Busy Judge

There once was a judge who was very busy. A woman whose husband had died kept coming to the judge for help. She had a problem that needed solving. Someone was bothering her. She wanted to know what the judge would do about her problem.

At first, the judge said he was too busy to help the woman. But she kept coming back again and again. She kept disturbing the judge. Finally, he knew he would never get anything done until he listened to her. He listened to her problem and settled it for her once and for all.

—Adapted from Luke 18:1–8

The message in this parable is about God. God is not like the busy judge. God always listens to us. We should turn to God often in prayer, asking Him to help us and thanking Him for all He has given us.

When we pray for something and we do not receive what we prayed for, it is not because God did not hear us or was too busy to help us. It is because God knows what is best for us. We have to learn to trust in God.

In our minds we can think about how much God loves us and remember that He will always care for us.

Read the following parable. In this parable the message is about ourselves and others.

The Proud Man and the Tax Collector

Two men went to a synagogue to pray. One of these men was a Pharisee. He kept all the rules completely, no matter what. He was more concerned about rules than about really loving God. The other man was a tax collector. Sometimes he cheated people. No one liked him very much.

The Pharisee stood tall and proud in the front of the synagogue. He made sure everyone could see and hear him. He prayed loudly, saying, "Thank you, God, for not making me like other people, especially not like that tax collector. I fast twice a week, and I give some of my money to the poor." On and on he prayed, bragging and boasting about himself and pointing out what others do wrong.

The tax collector, however, stood quietly in the back. He kept his head bowed low, not even raising his eyes to heaven. When he prayed, he said, "O God, be merciful to me, a sinner."
—Adapted from Luke 18:10–14

The message of this parable is about ourselves and others. God knows what we have done. We should not brag about the good things we do, or feel important because we have helped others. We please God by thanking Him for all He has given us. We should tell God how much we love Him. We need to ask God to help and guide us to be the best images of God we can be. If we have made wrong choices, we should tell God we are sorry and ask Him to help us not to do wrong again.

In our minds we can think about ourselves and others. Do we brag or think we are better than other people? We should remember that all people are made in the image of God, and that God loves all people.

WORD SCRAMBLE

Think about the following words. Unscramble these words. Write the correct word next to the scrambled word. Remember what you have learned about these words.

1. SEUJS _____

2. NIHKT _____

3. MBREREME _____

4. IDMN _____

5. RAYP _____

6. HORTSE _____

7. VLSEROSUE _____

8. ODLRW _____

9. OGD _____

10. EGMAIS _____

11. LETCSO _____

12. REPASBAL _____

In the following parable the message is about the world.

The Watchful Servants

A man is going on a trip. He leaves his home and places his servants in charge. All his servants know what their jobs are. They know what work to do while the man is gone. The man asks the servant at the gate to watch the house carefully.

The servants and the man at the gate should do the best that they can at their jobs, even when the owner of the house is away.
— Adapted from Mark 13:34–37

The message in this parable is about the world. Sometimes we are asked to be "in charge" of ourselves. Sometimes we are left alone in the classroom when the teacher has to leave for a few minutes. Sometimes we are left alone at home or in a store. How should we act? Do we always act as we should? There are times when things in the world distract us from acting as we should.

Sometimes our friends might distract us. When the teacher is out of the room, fooling around might look like fun. Sometimes things distract us. At home alone we might want to watch something on TV that we know we are not allowed to watch. In a store, a treat might look too good to pass up, and we might want to take it. We must think and remember what Jesus taught us.

In our minds we can think about how an image of God would act and remember to ask God to help us act as we should.

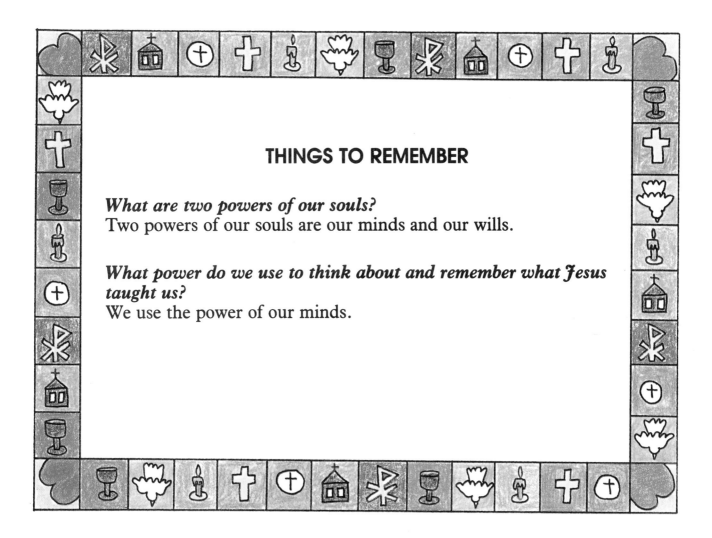

THINGS TO REMEMBER

What are two powers of our souls?
Two powers of our souls are our minds and our wills.

What power do we use to think about and remember what Jesus taught us?
We use the power of our minds.

6 God Gives Us the Power to Choose

WORDS TO KNOW

choose: To decide; to make a choice.
will: A power of the soul with which we make choices.

People are special. They are made in the image of God. As images of God we have wills to make choices. People can choose to live in houses, apartments, or tents. They can choose to work various hours—night or day. People can choose to eat anything from pizza to roast duck.

Animals do not have wills and cannot make choices as we do. God made animals to act in certain ways at certain times. Animals cannot choose how to act or what to do. They do the same things at the same times to survive. For example, all bears take shelter in dens, they hibernate all winter, and they eat berries.

Each and every day we make choices. Some choices are based on what we like (flavor of ice cream), some are based on what we need (food, clothing), and others are based on what we should do as images of God (following the Ten Commandments).

List five foods that you like to eat; five things you need to feel good and be healthy; and five ways you can act as an image of God.

Like	Need	Image of God
1. _____	1. _____	1. _____
2. _____	2. _____	2. _____
3. _____	3. _____	3. _____
4. _____	4. _____	4. _____
5. _____	5. _____	5. _____

As human beings, we make choices every day. The power to make choices exists within all of us. We call this power the will.

Below you will find five different situations. What choice would you make in each situation? Why?

1. You are invited to a party at your friend's house. Your friend's parents leave the house. While they are gone, a PG-rated movie is put in the VCR. Your parents have told you not to watch a PG movie without their permission. What should you do?

   a) Stay and watch the movie even though you know you should get your parents' permission first.

   b) Call your parents and ask your parents to come and take you home.

2. Your Dad asks you to rake the yard on a Saturday afternoon, and you agree to do it. As you are raking, some friends ride by on their bikes and ask you to play with them. What should you do?

   a) Stay and rake the leaves as you promised.

   b) Go with your friends and have fun.

3. You are walking down the aisle in a grocery store, and you see an open bag of candy. What should you do?

   a) Tell a person who works in the store what you found.

   b) Take a few pieces of candy, because nobody will ever know.

4. You and your friends are deciding to play a game. You need to choose teams. After teams have been chosen, there is one extra person. What should you do?

   a) Tell that person that he or she cannot play, because the teams will be uneven and unfair.

   b) Make room for the person on one of the teams.

5. You have a test that you need to take in one of your classes. What should you do?

   a) Study so that you do a *super* job on it.

   b) Don't study, because you think it will be easy.

It is a little scary when you have to make an important decision and you do not know which way to turn. Remember, you never make a decision alone. You have Jesus as a guide.

An easy rule to follow when making an important decision is to take these three steps first:

1. Listen to what other people have to say—for example, your parents, teachers, parish priests, and religious sisters.

2. Think about the situation and ask yourself what Jesus would do.

3. Pray to Jesus to help you make the right decision.

Because God has given each of us the gift of a free will, we can change our choices if we need or want to.

Sometimes we make the right choice and get hurt. At times we make the wrong choice and get by. We should try to make the right decisions. We should try to choose to do what Jesus would choose to do. This is always the right choice to make whether it makes us feel good or not.

Any time that we need to make a choice, we should ask ourselves:

Would Jesus do this?

> If not, we should not do it.
> If so, then it is something we may do
> or possibly should do.

Look back over the five situations and ask yourself the question:

Would Jesus do this?

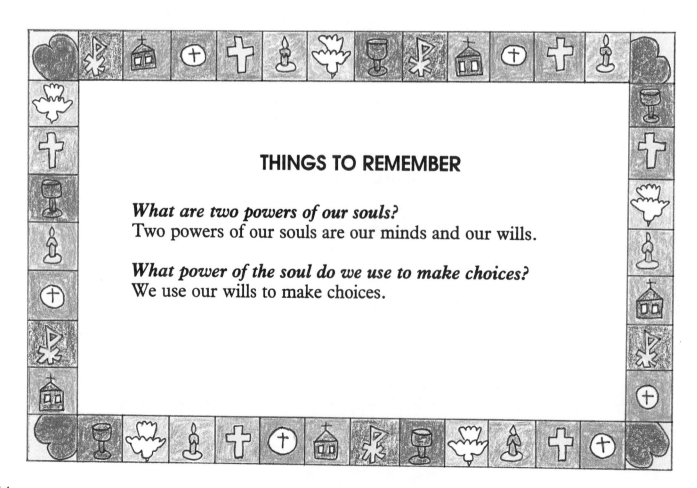

THINGS TO REMEMBER

What are two powers of our souls?
Two powers of our souls are our minds and our wills.

What power of the soul do we use to make choices?
We use our wills to make choices.

In the following parable, one son made the wrong choice because it was easier. The other made the wrong choice but decided to do what Jesus would do and changed his mind.

The Parable of the Two Sons

There was a man who had two sons. He came to the first and said, "Son, go out and work in the vineyard today."

The son replied, "I will not", but afterward he changed his mind and went and worked in the vineyard.

The man came to his other son and gave the same order. This son replied, "Yes, sir", but he did not go into the vineyard.
—Adapted from Matthew 21:28–32

7 God Gives Us Life

Words to Know

soul: The invisible, spiritual, and immortal gift from God that gives us life.

spiritual: Something you cannot see; not material.

immortal: Living forever.

God has given each of us a will to make choices and a mind with which to think. The will and the mind are powers of our souls. The soul is a wonderful gift from God. We cannot see our souls. They are invisible. We each have a soul that gives us life and enables us to share God's life, grace. Our souls live forever.

The human soul and the body together make up a living human being. Our souls give us life. We cannot live without our souls.

Imagine a wagon. It would not be a wagon without the four wheels. If we took the wheels away, the wagon would not roll. It would only drag. In this poor condition, the wagon would not last very long. A wagon without wheels is not a wagon. Without our souls, our bodies would not have life.

Our souls are the spiritual and immortal part of us. Our souls will never die. Even though our bodies die, our souls live on forever. They are immortal.

When people die, their bodies are not alive anymore. When people die, their souls leave their bodies. Their bodies are buried in the earth. If the person has acted as an image of God, then the person's soul goes to heaven. The person will live forever with God in heaven. We believe that when Jesus comes again, at the end of time, the bodies and souls of all the people who have died will come together again.

Our souls are immortal. That means our souls will live forever. To help understand how long forever is, think about the number of leaves on one tree. Add that number to the number of leaves on all the other trees in the world. Forever is more days than that. Forever is longer than we can ever imagine. We should always try to act as images of God, so that we can live forever with God in heaven.

Thinking with our minds helps us learn things. In order to learn we must listen. One way to learn about God and how to act as an image of God is to listen to what the Bible teaches and to listen to what the Church teaches. Our parents, teachers, and priests tell us what the Bible and the Church teach. We should listen to them and learn.

When we make right choices with our wills, we act as images of God. We make the right choices when we follow Jesus' example. Jesus gives us grace to help us make right choices.

We can think because we have minds. We can make choices because we have wills. If we think about God with our minds and make right choices with our wills, we will live as images of God here on earth and someday live forever with God in heaven.

Read the story below about a saint who used the two most important powers of the soul, thinking and choosing, to show his love for God and others.

St. Thomas Aquinas

Thomas was born a long time ago in the year 1225, in a little village in the country of Italy. He was a very well-behaved and happy little boy. He often thought and wondered about God.

It was the custom, in those days, that, when a boy turned five years old, he was sent away to school to study. When Thomas was five, he was sent to a famous monastery, where he began a life of prayer and study.

At first, Thomas was frightened and lonely, because he had never before been away from home. Eventually, Thomas came to love the monastery, because there he seemed to be closer to God. He believed that he should become a priest or a brother.

During this time in Italy, wars were going on. During the wars, soldiers took over the monastery; so Thomas did not return to school there. But after Thomas grew up, he attended college at the University of Naples. There, Thomas met a well-known priest. This priest belonged to a group of people who tried to live a good life by following the example of St. Dominic. Members of this group of people are called Dominicans. Thomas liked what this priest did. Thomas wanted to become a Dominican, too.

Thomas applied to join the Dominicans and was accepted. Thomas' mother became very angry, because she did not think that living the life of a Dominican was good enough for her son. Thomas did not want to go against his mother's wishes, but he felt it was more important to follow God's call.

While Thomas was on his way to live with the Dominicans, his own brothers came and kidnapped him. They took him back home, where his mother locked him in his room.

Months went by. Thomas remained locked in his room. His sisters brought him food and tried to persuade him not to join the Dominicans. Thomas' brothers tried tempting him to commit sins, but God protected Thomas. Thomas made the right choices. Thomas was helped by thinking often about God.

After a while, Thomas escaped. Then he joined the Dominican priests in Naples. Thomas declared that he did not want to serve anyone other than God. In January 1245, Thomas made his promise to live his life as a Dominican. He began his studies to become a priest. He studied very hard and continued to pray often.

After five years of studying, Thomas was ordained a priest. This was the happiest time of his life. However, during that same year something happened to make Thomas very sad. His two brothers and his mother died. Thomas was so sad that he cried often.

Thomas went on to become a teacher at a college. Even though his life was very busy with studying, teaching, preaching, and helping others, Thomas always found time for prayer.

In 1272, Thomas became very sick. His illness left him quite weak, but he continued to teach and to preach the word of God. Two years later, Thomas became ill again. This time he died.

Some years later, Thomas was declared a saint. We celebrate his feast day on January 28. Thomas gave his life to God and others as a priest and teacher. Thomas used the powers of his soul well. Thomas thought about God often. With God's help, Thomas made the right choices. As a saint he lives with God forever in heaven. St. Thomas Aquinas is a good example for us to follow.

THINGS TO REMEMBER

What is the soul?
The soul is the invisible, spiritual, and immortal gift from God that gives us life.

What are two powers of our souls?
Two powers of our souls are our minds and wills.

What power do we use to think about and remember what Jesus taught us?
We use the power of our minds to think about and remember what Jesus taught.

What power do we use to make choices?
We use the power of our wills to make choices.

8 All Persons Have Dignity

WORDS TO KNOW

dignity: Worthy of respect.
traditional: Doing things as they were done in the past.
village: Small town.
thatch: Straw.
scarce: Rare, hard to find, not common.
responsibility: Duty; job.
self-esteem: Self-respect.

We are images of God. We are all persons. As persons, we have dignity. As persons, we are worthy of respect.

One person does not have more dignity than another person. People can and do have different abilities, likes, and dislikes. But their dignity remains the same. As images of God, we all have the same boundless worth and value.

Two boys, James and John, are both third-graders. They are in the same class. Both boys are very good students. They seem to be very much alike. Yet their families are very different. James' family owns many things. John's family does not. This difference bothers John.

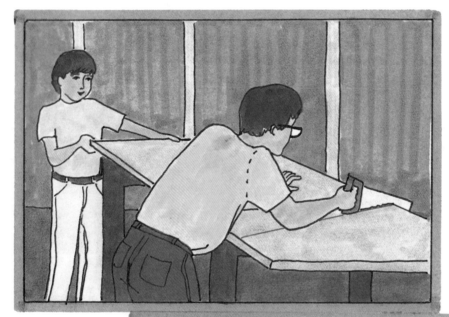

*John
and
his
dad*

*James
and
his
dad*

James and John

James: My dad owns ten department stores. He has a chauffeur who drives him to work in a limousine every day.

John: My dad is a carpenter. He makes things in our basement.

James: My mom loves to shop. She has a credit card for every store. She also has a closet full of beautiful clothes.

John: My mom enjoys staying home. She makes all of our meals from scratch and decorates our house with beautiful homemade crafts. She even has time to play ball with me and help me with my homework.

James: My older brother Tim has his own car. Dad pays for the gas and insurance. Tim drives his friends to school every day.

John: My brother Mike helps Dad fix our old station wagon. It's the only car we have. Mike rarely uses it with his friends.

James: I have my own TV, VCR, computer, and telephone.

John: We have a small TV in the family room.

James: You don't have much, do you.

John: No.

James: Wouldn't you rather be rich like me?

John: Well, I guess so, but I love my family. We're all healthy and happy. Things just don't mean that much to us. James, we both deserve respect, not for how much we have, but for who we are—images of God.

James: I guess you're right. As persons, everyone has dignity.

Like all of us, James was born with dignity. When he does not act as an image of God and brags too much, he does not lose his dignity. It is just harder for us to see.

John does not lose his dignity by being envious, either. His dignity is just not clearly seen. Acting as images of God makes their dignity clearer to see.

All persons have dignity, not because of what they own but because of who they are—images of God. All persons should be treated with respect.

As persons, we have dignity. All human persons in all of the other parts of the world have dignity, too.

The nation of Tonga is made up of 150 islands. It is located about one thousand miles north of New Zealand.

Most of the people are farmers. They like to live a traditional way of life.

Nuku (*noo-koo*) is a happy nine-year-old girl. She lives in a small house with a thatch roof, along with her two brothers and two sisters. All of the children in Tonga attend school until they are fourteen years old.

In the morning, Nuku's father works in the garden; and in the afternoon, he fishes for tuna and shark. Nuku's mother does the housework and sometimes helps in the garden.

After school, Nuku and her friends enjoy playing hide-and-seek among the trees and swinging on the vines that hang from the branches. Sometimes, they create their own play villages with handmade dolls, houses, and furniture.

In school, they read about life in other places. Some of the children they read about live in big houses, play with store-bought toys, and ride in fancy cars.

The children of Tonga do not have these things. This does not bother Nuku, her family, or her friends. The people of Tonga understand that people are more important than things. They respect each other's dignity. They act as images of God. Their dignity is easy to see.

Many people want to visit Tonga because of the warm friendliness of the people. One tourist, a representative of the United States, invited Nuku to live and attend school in the United States for one year.

Nuku did not want to go, at first. She loved her home. But the chance to visit new people in a new place excited her. She accepted the invitation. At the end of the summer, she left for Minneapolis, Minnesota.

After the thrill of the plane ride and the excitement of seeing the large city of Minneapolis for the first time, Nuku finds it hard to get used to life in the United States. Material things seem so important to the people here. Children live in large houses, they ride in fancy cars, and some of them even have their own bedrooms and spending money. It seems to Nuku that children with the most things are the most popular.

At home on Tonga, money is scarce. Nuku wears her clothes until she outgrows them. She does not get new clothes very often. When she does need new clothes, her mother makes them for her. The family house her father built has two rooms for seven people. The family does not need a car. Because they live on a farm in the village, everything they need is within walking distance.

Family life is so important on Tonga. Nuku has responsibilities at home. She cares for her younger brothers and sisters, helps with the housework, and helps prepare meals.

Here in the United States, her self-esteem is very low. She doesn't have all the things that the popular girls have. She doesn't do the things she used to do back home. She has very little pride in herself. She has forgotten who she is and what is important to her.

Nuku knows that she is going to be in Minneapolis for a long time. She must talk to someone about her problem. She asks Susan, the daughter of the family she is living with, to meet her after school in the park so they can be alone to talk.

When they meet in the park, Nuku says to Susan, "I've lost the good feeling I used to have about myself. I don't have all of the things to be popular. I don't do the things I used to do back home. I look different from everyone else; my clothes are different; I even talk differently."

Susan said, "Every person is different on the outside. On the inside, every person is made in the image of God. We should be proud of who we are."

"If everyone is an image of God," said Nuku, "then why do so many of the kids make fun of me and treat me like I'm not?"

Susan said, "Unfortunately, people do not always act as the persons they were created to be. Some people do not treat others as kindly as they should. Some people do not respect the dignity of others."

Nuku said, "I feel as if I don't deserve respect."

"As a person, you have dignity!" said Susan. "You *do* deserve respect! When people treat you unkindly, you need to hold your head high and be proud of who you are! Tell other people about life on Tonga. Tell them that people on Tonga know that persons are more important than things, and that acting as images of God is the most important thing of all."

Nuku said, "Thanks, Susan. You've really been a help. You are a good friend."

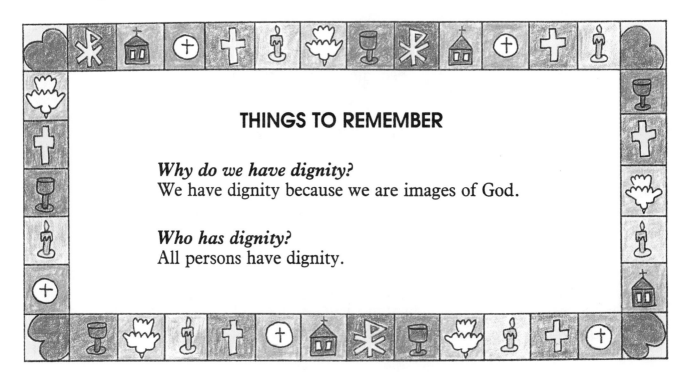

THINGS TO REMEMBER

Why do we have dignity?
We have dignity because we are images of God.

Who has dignity?
All persons have dignity.

Unit 3: Acting as Images of God

9 How We Should Act

WORDS TO KNOW

shepherd: One who takes care of sheep.
advisors: People who give advice or information.
prophet: One who speaks for God.
Scripture: Holy writings about God.
test: Proof of ability or skill.
govern: To take care of.

Following Christ the King and acting as an image of God is not an easy job. Sometimes it involves resisting temptation.

In the following story, Jesus was tempted by the devil but did not give in. He showed us how to resist temptation.

The Temptation

One day, Jesus went into the desert to fast and pray. He had very little to eat for forty days and forty nights. He was feeling weak. The devil knew that Jesus must be hungry, so he tempted Jesus to turn some stones into bread so that Jesus could have something to eat.

The devil wanted Jesus to show off. He wanted Jesus to use His power as God to change stones into bread. Jesus said, "One does not live by bread alone, but by every word that comes forth from the mouth of God." When Jesus spoke those words, He was telling us that we need more than food to live a good life. We also need God's words of love to guide us.

The devil and Jesus were on the roof of the temple. The devil said, "If you are the Son of God, throw yourself down." The devil then said that God would send His angels to protect Jesus. The devil told Jesus: "With their hands they will support you." In other words, the devil was tempting Jesus to test God. Jesus answered, "You shall not put the Lord, your God, to the test." With those words, Jesus was telling us that we should believe in what God says because God always tells the truth.

Finally, the devil and Jesus were on a very high mountain, and the devil showed Jesus all the kingdoms of the world. The devil told Jesus that all these things would be His if He would fall on His knees and worship the devil. Jesus answered: "Get away, Satan!" Jesus told the devil that persons should worship only God.

The devil left Jesus, and angels came and waited on Him.

—Adapted from Matthew 4:1–11

Resisting temptation as Jesus did is a very good way to practice acting as an image of God. It is a way of following Christ the King.

The King Who Changed His Ways

There was a king who ruled over a large kingdom. He loved to give orders from his throne in the palace. Every day he would make new rules that were unfair to the people of his kingdom.

For example, one day the king announced: "Bicycles and cars are no longer allowed on the streets. The people of my kingdom must walk backward."

The townspeople were angry when they heard the news. But they knew that they must do what the king commanded. So everyone in town began to walk backward.

Meanwhile, the king was spending time alone in his castle garden, looking at his favorite plants. His servants did not know he was out in the garden, so they locked the castle gates.

The king had no key. He was locked out of his castle! He pounded on the large doors, but no one could hear him. He decided to drive into town to get some help.

82

At a stop sign, a policeman told him that he was not supposed to be driving in the town by order of the king. The king cried, "But I am the king!" The policeman did not believe him and took away his car.

It didn't take the king long to notice that everyone was walking backward. People shouted at him, "Turn around!" He shouted back, "But I am the king!" No one would believe him.

For two days the king had to stay in town and follow his own silly orders. He hated having to do so.

His servants finally came to town looking for him. He was so glad to see them that he made a promise. "I am going to get rid of these awful rules. I am going to see what rules my people need to lead happy lives. Those are the rules I will make, and I will help the people keep them."

From that day forward, the king was a true king. He made only fair rules and helped the people of his kingdom.

We just read that a true king is someone who knows what is right for his people and does it. Christ was a true king. He knew what was right and He did it. Jesus showed us how to act.

Following Christ the King and acting as an image of God is not an easy job. Sometimes it involves resisting temptation.

In the Bible story "The Temptation", Jesus was tempted by the devil but did not give in. He showed us how to resist temptation.

Resisting temptation as Jesus did is a very good way to practice acting as an image of God. It is a way of following Christ the King.

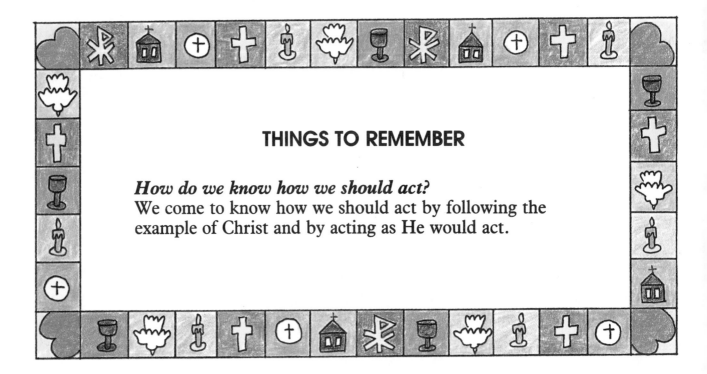

THINGS TO REMEMBER

How do we know how we should act?
We come to know how we should act by following the example of Christ and by acting as He would act.

10 Loving God and Others: The Ten Commandments

WORDS TO KNOW

dreaded: Feared.

bitter: Unpleasant.

mortar: A clay and water mixture used to make bricks.

slavery: Treating people as property.

subjects: Those under the rule of a king.

witness: Person who has seen or heard something.

worship: Respect and honor to God.

conversation: Talking; sharing information.

in vain: Without respect.

true: Genuine; right; correct; the only one.

Sabbath: The Lord's day; the day we go to Mass.

honor: Respect.

errand: Job.

attack: Grab, harm.

dignity: Worth, value.

friendship: Being friends; caring about each other.

trust: To have confidence in someone and to be able to count on that person when you need help.

truth: Something true or right.

covet: To want to take for yourself what others have.

steal: To take something that does not belong to you.

adultery: To try to love in a married way someone we are not married to.

bear false witness: Lie.

Thousands of years ago, before Jesus was born, a special group of people called the Israelites lived in Egypt. The number of Israelite families was large. The Israelites were successful and happy.

The Egyptian Pharaoh (or king) was worried that the Israelites might someday take over Egypt. He encouraged the Egyptian people to do something about them.

The Egyptians were afraid of the Israelites because there were so many of them. So the Egyptians decided to make life unpleasant for them by forcing them to become slaves. As slaves, they had to work with mortar to make bricks and work in the fields.

The Pharaoh commanded all of his subjects, "Throw into the river every boy that is born to the Hebrews [Israelites], but you may let all the girls live." He did this so that the number of Israelite families would be fewer.
—Adapted from Exodus 1:12–14, 22

The Calling of Moses

A baby boy was born to a Hebrew woman. The mother saved him from being killed by hiding him from the Pharaoh's men for three months. When she could hide him no longer, she placed him in a basket and hid it among the reeds near the river, hoping that someone would come along and find him and care for him.

Pharaoh's daughter was taking a bath in the river when she saw the basket among the reeds. On opening the basket, she found the baby boy, crying! She kept the baby and cared for him.

When the baby grew older, the Pharaoh's daughter adopted him and called him "Moses", which means "I drew him out of the water".

As Moses grew, he witnessed the harsh treatment of the Israelite people by the Egyptians. He wanted to do something about it, but he didn't know what to do.

The Pharaoh heard about Moses' wish and ordered him to be put to death. But Moses escaped to another country.

While in that country, Moses heard God call out to him from a burning bush. When Moses understood that God was speaking to him, he hid his face because he was afraid.

God told Moses that He knew about the suffering people in Egypt. God asked Moses to be the one to lead them out of Egypt to a better place. God also promised to stay with Moses and the Israelites throughout their journey.

Moses did what God asked him to do. The journey was long and hard.

Three months after leaving Egypt, the Israelites arrived at the foot of Mount Sinai. God asked Moses to come to the top of the mountain. Moses climbed the mountain to meet God.

There, at the top of the mountain, God gave Moses the Ten Commandments so that the Israelite people would know how God acts and how they should act as images of God. These commandments were written down on stone tablets and taken down the mountain by Moses to the Israelites below.

—Adapted from Exodus 2:1–4:17, 12:37–20:17

We learned that God gave Moses the Ten Commandments on Mount Sinai. The Ten Commandments tell us how God acts and how we should act as images of God. The first three commandments tell us about God and how we should love Him. (The commandments are based on Exodus 20:2–17 and Deuteronomy 5:6–21.)

I. I am the Lord, your God. You will not have other gods besides Me.

II. You will not take the name of the Lord your God in vain.

III. Remember to keep holy the Sabbath day.

In the first commandment, God is telling us that He is the Creator; the only Being deserving of our worship. God is asking us to love Him and worship only Him.

By the choices we make with our free wills, we can choose to love and worship God through prayer and sacrifice.

When we pray, we talk to God. We should give Him our full attention. A prayer is not only some words we have memorized and repeat when we awake in the morning, before our meals, and before bedtime. Prayer is a conversation with God. We thank Him for what we have, ask Him to watch over us and guide us, tell Him we are sorry for our wrong choices, and praise Him.

A sacrifice is a gift. It is not something we can place in a box and wrap. It is the gift of ourselves. It is giving of ourselves, our time, and our talents.

Sometimes we are asked to do things we do not like to do. It is hard to accept a job willingly without complaining. Doing a job without complaining and without being told is a sacrifice.

God asks us to help others when we can. When your mother needs help with the dishes, you should pitch in and help. When someone falls, we should help the person up and try to make the person feel better. When unkind words are spoken, we should disagree and not repeat them.

Remember, other people are images of God, too. Whatever we do for others, we do for God.

God has done a lot for us. We should love Him most of all, be thankful for what He has given us, and expect nothing in return. Even though we should expect nothing in return from God for our love, God does always love us and care for us.

God is not like a television set. That is, we do not turn Him on when we want something and then turn Him off when we think we have everything we need.

Instead, we should be "tuned in" to God all the time. He likes to hear from us every day. He deserves our respect and praise.

The second commandment tells us: "You will not take the name of the Lord your God in vain." A name is like a person's title. It stands for that person. The way we use a name indicates what we think of that person.

God's name should always be used with respect. When we use His name with love in prayers and songs, we are giving Him that respect. When we use God's name while angry or to comment on something we do not like, we are not giving Him that respect. We are using God's name "in vain", which means without respect. We are using God's name in the wrong way. We should not use God's name in the wrong way.

The third commandment tells us: "Remember to keep holy the Sabbath day." The Sabbath day, or the Lord's day, is a day of worship and rest. To keep it holy means to give the day to God.

In order to follow the third commandment, we should remember that Sunday is a day of rest. We should finish most of our work during the week and save Sunday for Mass, fun, and family. When we do not spend time with our families, work too hard, or skip Mass on Sunday, we are not following the third commandment.

The first three commandments tell us about God and how we, as images of God, should love God. Using the "code" given below, write the first three commandments. Then, under each commandment, write what the commandment means.

Code: Write the letter of the alphabet that comes *before* the one that is given.

<pre>
 __   __ __   __ __ __   __ __ __ __
 J   B N   U I F   M P S E,

 __ __ __ __   __ __ __   __ __ __
 Z P V S   H P E.   Z P V

 __ __ __ __   __ __ __   __ __ __ __
 X J M M   O P U   I B W F

 __ __ __ __ __   __ __ __ __
 P U I F S   H P E T

 __ __ __ __ __ __ __   __ __
 C F T J E F T   N F.
</pre>

$\overline{Z}$ $\overline{P}$ $\overline{V}$ $\overline{X}$ $\overline{J}$ $\overline{M}$ $\overline{M}$ $\overline{O}$ $\overline{P}$ $\overline{U}$

$\overline{U}$ $\overline{B}$ $\overline{L}$ $\overline{F}$ $\overline{U}$ $\overline{I}$ $\overline{F}$ $\overline{O}$ $\overline{B}$ $\overline{N}$ $\overline{F}$

$\overline{P}$ $\overline{G}$ $\overline{U}$ $\overline{I}$ $\overline{F}$ $\overline{M}$ $\overline{P}$ $\overline{S}$ $\overline{E}$

$\overline{Z}$ $\overline{P}$ $\overline{V}$ $\overline{S}$ $\overline{H}$ $\overline{P}$ $\overline{E}$

$\overline{J}$ $\overline{O}$ $\overline{W}$ $\overline{B}$ $\overline{J}$ $\overline{O}$.

$\overline{S}$ $\overline{F}$ $\overline{N}$ $\overline{F}$ $\overline{N}$ $\overline{C}$ $\overline{F}$ $\overline{S}$ $\overline{U}$ $\overline{P}$

$\overline{L}$ $\overline{F}$ $\overline{F}$ $\overline{Q}$ $\overline{I}$ $\overline{P}$ $\overline{M}$ $\overline{Z}$ $\overline{U}$ $\overline{I}$ $\overline{F}$

$\overline{T}$ $\overline{B}$ $\overline{C}$ $\overline{C}$ $\overline{B}$ $\overline{U}$ $\overline{I}$ $\overline{E}$ $\overline{B}$ $\overline{Z}$.

In the last seven commandments, God tells us how to love ourselves and others the way He loves us and others. As images of God, we should act the way He acts.

The fourth commandment, "Honor your father and your mother", tells us that God loves parents. He gives them the responsibility to love and care for children.

Love is shown in the care that parents provide, the guiding words that they speak, and the good actions that they perform. Parents express care for their children by providing food, clothing, shelter, education, and spiritual guidance for them.

Loving parents would never ask their children to do something that is not God-like, something that is harmful. They would never keep from their children the food, clothing, shelter, or education that they need. Loving parents would never keep their children from prayer or religious education, either.

This commandment tells all children to do what their parents ask. Children should listen to their parents, come when they are called by their parents, help their parents around the house, and help their parents care for younger brothers and sisters. When children do not listen to their parents and help them when they should, the children are not following the fourth commandment.

Adult children are asked to love and respect their parents, too. This love can be shown by running errands for parents, helping them when they are sick, visiting them, and praying for them.

The fifth commandment is: "You will not kill." We are asked in the fifth commandment to act with kindness toward everyone. This commandment tells us not to hurt or harm anyone, including ourselves. Remember, God loves and cares for all human life, all persons born and unborn. As images of God, we should do the same.

Caring for ourselves includes eating properly, dressing properly, and watching what we do. Eating too much or too little food, or wearing improper clothing, can make us sick. Pills that we are not supposed to take can make us sick. The body is a special gift—it is part of us as images of God. Treat it with care.

Acting with kindness means we should not hit others or treat them badly. An attack on a human body is an attack on a human person, because the human body is part of us. Every human body has the same dignity and value that our own bodies have. We do not want someone to hit us; therefore, we should not hit someone else.

In the sixth commandment, "You will not commit adultery", God tells us that people should love one another as God loves them.

A good friendship between two people involves a special kind of love. Both people like each other. They trust each other. They depend on each other.

Marriage is a special kind of friendship and love between a husband and wife. On their wedding day, a man and a woman promise to love each other in a particular way, to trust each other, and to depend on each other for help.

Sometimes it is not easy for a husband and wife to do what they promised. While still married, husbands or wives might decide to find someone else to try to love in this special way. This is called adultery.

We must pray for these people. They are no longer doing what they promised. They are not following the sixth commandment.

Even though none of you are married, you are still asked to follow the sixth commandment. You should make promises only if you can keep them, and you should love as God loves.

The sixth commandment also asks us to respect the dignity of other persons' bodies. Sometimes movies or books and magazines show people improperly dressed, using the wrong language, and treating each other poorly. These movies and books are not respecting the dignity of these persons' bodies.

When we do not take care of our bodies by dressing properly, we are not following the sixth commandment. When we watch movies or look at books or magazines that show people who are improperly dressed, we are not following the sixth commandment.

The seventh commandment says: "You will not steal." Stealing means taking something that belongs to someone else. Damaging something you have borrowed or not returning it is wrong, too. Persons who love each other respect each other's property. We should show our love for other people by not stealing.

When God created the world and us, He invited each of us to take care of some of the things in our world. These things include our personal possessions and anything we use or borrow. In giving us these things, God shows His love for all people. We should love all people as God does, by taking care of the things of the world.

God has given us a beautiful world to enjoy. We are responsible for it and must take care of it. Damaging trees and lakes is destroying gifts from God.

God always tells the truth. As images of God, we should tell the truth, too.

The eighth commandment tells us, "You will not bear false witness against your neighbor." To "bear false witness" means to lie. When we lie to another person or about another person, we do not love the truth. When we lie about another person, we are not respecting that person's dignity as an image of God. We are not loving as God loves.

Sometimes people make mistakes or have bad habits. We should not tell others about these mistakes or habits. If we know that someone is doing something harmful to himself or herself or to someone else, then we should tell someone in charge.

It is not easy being honest. We should stop and think before we speak or act, to make sure that we are being honest.

The ninth commandment tells us, "You will not covet your neighbor's wife." To "covet" means to want to take for yourself what others have.

God does not want to control us like robots, because He loves us. We have minds to think and wills to make choices. Sometimes people will choose to be friends, and sometimes they will not.

Just as God does not want to control us, we should not want to control others, either. We are asked to respect the freedom of others and not think of them as objects for our own enjoyment.

We learned from the sixth commandment that friendships are special. We enjoy our friends because we like them, we can trust them, and we can depend on them.

Sometimes we want to be a close friend to someone who is a close friend to someone else. We want that person to be our friend only and no one else's. We want to take that person's friendship for ourselves and not share it with anyone else.

When that happens, we need to remember that everyone has a free will to make choices. We must respect other persons' freedom and not think of any person as an object to be owned.

Married people sometimes notice the gifts and talents of other people and wish they had married someone else. But they must remember to notice the gifts and talents that their husband or wife has. The more husbands and wives praise each other for the gifts they already have, the less they will wish that they had married someone else.

Because He loves us, God does not take and keep for Himself the things that He gave us. As images of God, we should not want to take what belongs to others, either.

The tenth commandment tells us: "You will not covet anything that belongs to your neighbor." This means that we should be happy for others when they own something that we would like to have. We should not be envious or unkind. God has given us the right to own things in this world. We should be satisfied with what we own.

Under each picture, write the number of the commandment that applies to it. Then circle "yes" if the people in the picture are following the commandment. Circle "no" if they are not following the commandment. Finally, write the commandment on the lines beneath the picture.

Commandment # _____
YES   NO
_____
_____

Commandment # _____
YES   NO
_____
_____

Commandment # _____
YES   NO
_____
_____

Commandment # _____
YES   NO
_____
_____

Commandment # _____
YES   NO
_____
_____

Commandment # _____
YES   NO
_____
_____

Commandment # _____

YES   NO

_____

_____

Commandment # _____

YES   NO

_____

_____

Commandment # _____

YES   NO

_____

_____

Commandment # _____

YES   NO

_____

_____

THINGS TO REMEMBER

How do we act as God acts?
We act as God acts by following the Ten Commandments.

11 We Become What We Do

WORDS TO KNOW

unreliable: Not trustworthy.
inconsiderate: Thoughtless.
parable: Short story with a religious lesson.
merchant: A buyer and seller of goods.
valuable: Having great worth or importance.
decision: Choice.
extraordinary: Unusual, remarkable.

When we think about something, choose to do it, and practice doing it, we become better performers of that act. It is easier for us to do that act.

For example, if we are constantly late, we become unreliable, and it is easier for us to continue being late. If we tell many lies, we become more untruthful, and it becomes easier for us to lie. If we are thoughtless and have no time for other people, we become more inconsiderate, and it is easier for us to act in a thoughtless way. As we can see, our actions and words are very important. We become what we do!

The parable of the Good Samaritan is a good example of how we become what we do. Pay careful attention to all of the characters!

The Good Samaritan

Narrator: A merchant from Jerusalem had some business to take care of in Jericho. He left the town early one morning. He thought to himself, "It looks like a beautiful day, and I have so many things to trade, sell, and buy. I should be able to reach Jericho by nightfall." Unfortunately, the merchant did not know that he had company waiting for him farther down the road.

100

Merchant: (*Some time later.*) I have covered many miles, and I am pleased. I hope the good weather holds up.

Leading Robber: (*Hiding behind a large boulder.*) Look at the things the merchant is carrying! They must be valuable! Let's get them!

Narrator: The robbers jumped on the man and beat him up. They took all of his things and left him almost dead.

Merchant: I feel so weak. I hope that someone will come along and help me before it's too late. Oh, look, a man, just down the road! His hands are folded in prayer. Surely he will help me!

Narrator: The man was praying quietly, his eyes focused only on the road in front of him. But out of the corner of his eye he noticed the wounded merchant.

Praying Man: How sad! The poor man must have been beaten. I'd like to stop, but I'll be late if I do. I must hurry on.

Merchant: It looks like there is no hope for me. But wait! Could that be another person coming down the road?

Narrator: It was another person. The sight of the wounded man caused him to stop suddenly.

Traveler: Oh, my gosh, how terrible! I don't know what to do. I know I should stay, but I'm frightened. I think I'd better be on my way.

Narrator: The merchant was so weak that he could not speak. He would surely die if no one came to help him. But someone did come, a person from Samaria. Unfortunately, the merchant and his countrymen were enemies of the Samaritan people. Would an enemy come to his aid?

Samaritan: How can this be? This man has been out here, all alone, for a long time, and no one has helped him. Here, friend, let me clean and wrap your wounds. I'll place you on my donkey and take you to a nearby inn.

Narrator: The Samaritan placed the merchant in a warm bed at the inn. He paid the innkeeper well and requested one more thing before he left.

Samaritan: Take good care of him, please. I will pay you back in full for any additional expenses when I return.

—Adapted from Luke 10:29–37

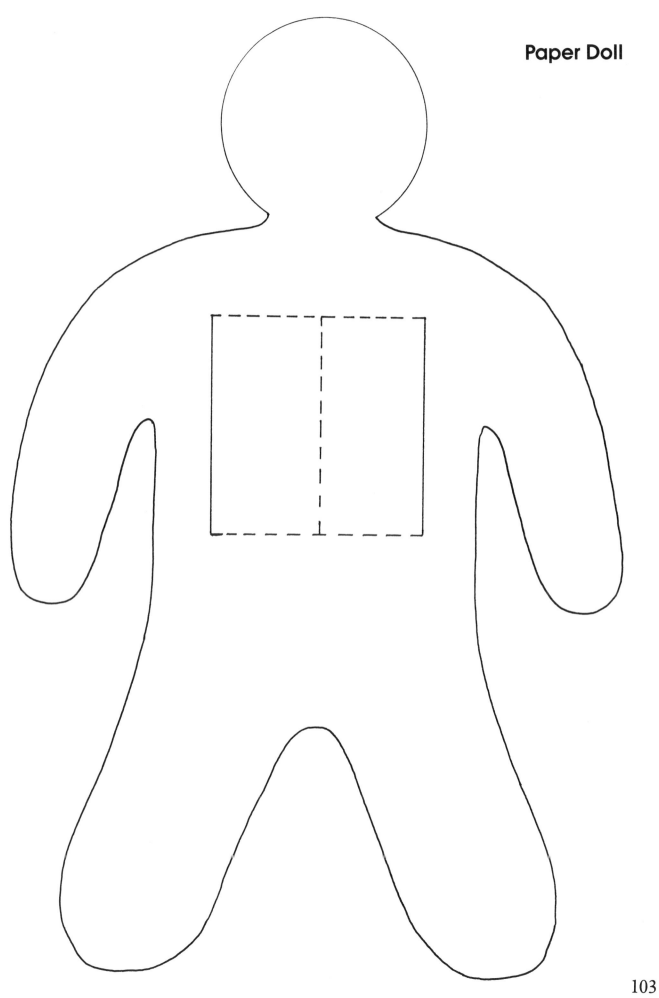

Paper Doll

103

Sometimes it seems as if only people who do fantastic, extraordinary things can become saints. Yet when we read about saints like Thérèse of Lisieux, we recognize that we can become holy by doing little things well. When we act like a saint, we become more saintly, and it is easier for us to act saintly. We become what we do. We become saints!

Thérèse, the Little Flower

Thérèse Martin was born in Lisieux, France, in 1873. As she grew older, she loved her parents more and more. She would pick wild flowers and bring them to her parents to show her love for them.

When she was fifteen years old, Thérèse became a nun. She remembered picking flowers for her parents as a young girl.

Thérèse compared her everyday actions to those flowers. Every time she scrubbed the floors, set the table, or washed clothes, it was as if she were picking a flower. She would then give this "flower" to God to show her love for Him.

When she died, she was only twenty-four years old. Yet her life was full because she offered all of her everyday actions to God. Thérèse thought about what an image of God should do and chose to do those things over and over again until she became the best image of God she could be. She became a saint.

Like Thérèse, we can think about what an image of God should do in our day-to-day activities. We can chose to do those things well. We can chose to do those things over and over again until we become the best images of God we can be. We become saints!

GREAT PLAYERS IN LIFE

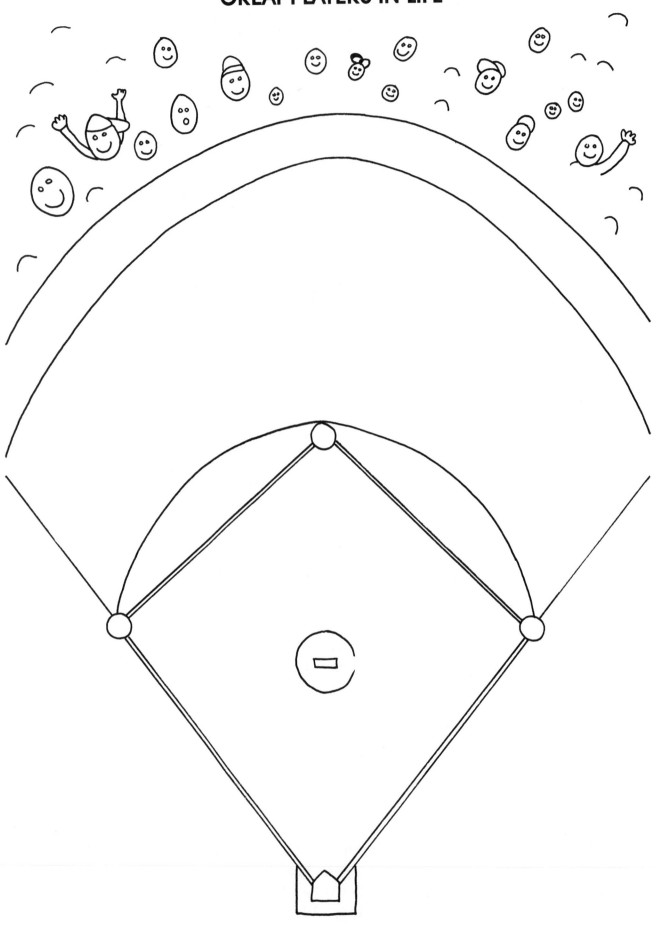

Ted makes fun of his teacher when she turns her back.

Sue raises her hand before speaking.

Even though Ken does not like math, he tries his best and asks for help.

Mary asks the new girl to jump rope with her.

Fred helps his teacher without being asked.

Eric teases a classmate because of his haircut.

Harold tells Jim that he can't play ball with the others because Jim isn't good enough.

Jamie chews on the pencil he borrowed, then gives it back.

Jane cuts in front of the other children in line.

Mark helps a classmate clean out his desk.

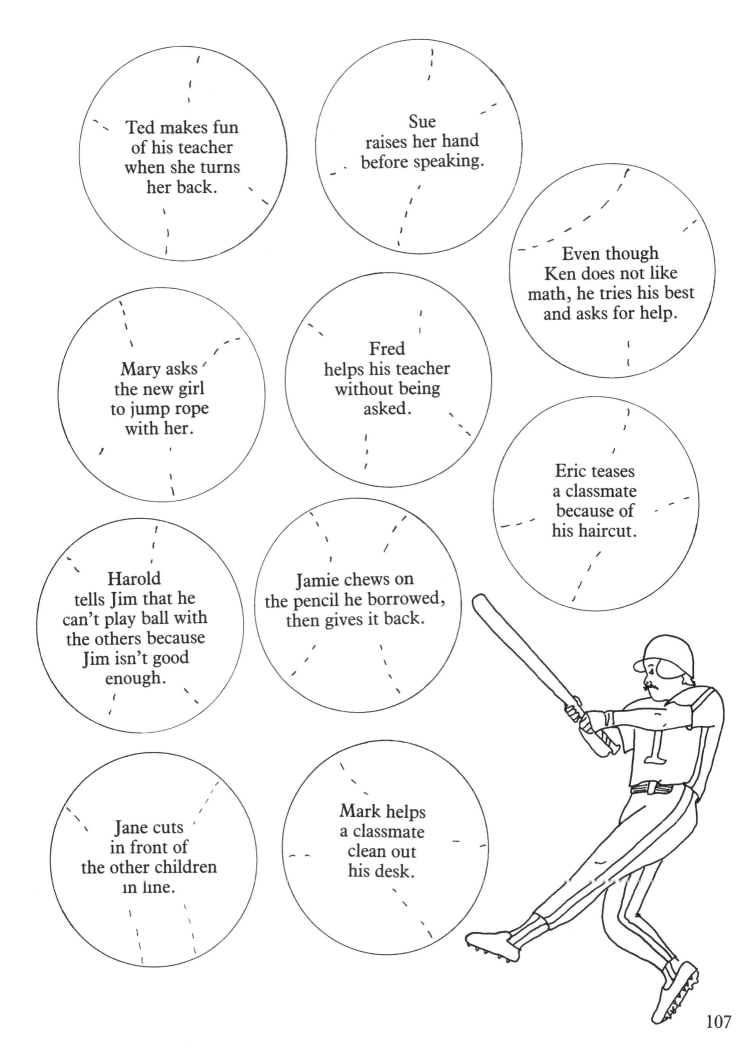

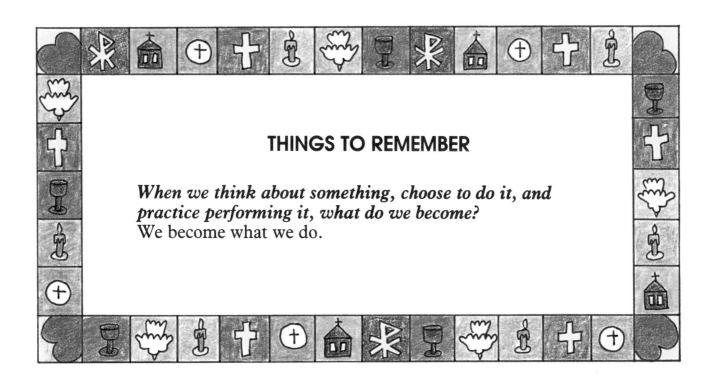

THINGS TO REMEMBER

When we think about something, choose to do it, and practice performing it, what do we become?
We become what we do.

12 Shaping Ourselves into Followers of Jesus

WORDS TO KNOW

fault: Bad habit, weakness.
imperfect: With fault.
transform: To change.

Sometimes we share outwardly the thoughts, choices, and feelings we have inside. When we are happy, we smile; when we are sad, we cry; when we want to show other persons that we love them, we give them a hug.

Our actions should reflect God's actions, but sometimes our faults get in the way. We do not act as images of God. Jesus is the perfect image of God the Father. If we want to change and become better images of God, we should become followers of Jesus. Our actions should be like His. Remember to think of Jesus before making decisions. He will help us know what to do, and He will help us make the right choice.

Write what you think Jesus would do in this difficult situation. If we want to follow Jesus, what should we do in this situation?

_____

_____

_____

_____

Think of difficult situations that might happen to third graders.
Write about one of them here. Tell what Jesus would do in this
situation and what we should do as followers of Jesus.

_____

_____

_____

_____

_____

_____

_____

_____

_____

_____

_____

_____

_____

_____

_____

_____

_____

_____

_____

_____

_____

It is often difficult for us to act as images of God. Jesus knows how difficult it is because He is human as well as the perfect image of God the Father. He suffered and died because He acted as the perfect image of God the Father. The Sorrowful Mysteries of the Rosary remind us of the terrible things that happened to Jesus.

When we face a difficult situation, we can think of the Sorrowful Mysteries. We should ask Jesus to help us with the difficult task we must do.

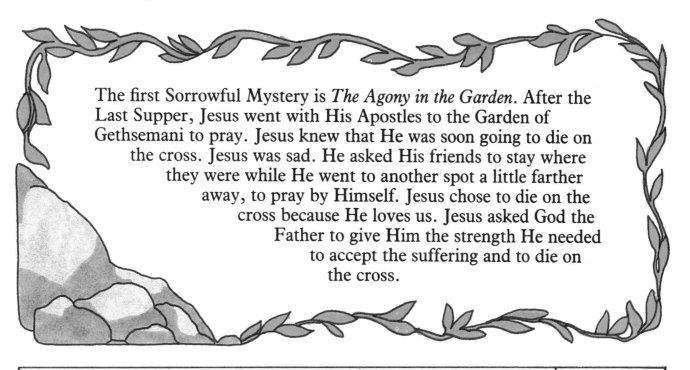

The first Sorrowful Mystery is *The Agony in the Garden*. After the Last Supper, Jesus went with His Apostles to the Garden of Gethsemani to pray. Jesus knew that He was soon going to die on the cross. Jesus was sad. He asked His friends to stay where they were while He went to another spot a little farther away, to pray by Himself. Jesus chose to die on the cross because He loves us. Jesus asked God the Father to give Him the strength He needed to accept the suffering and to die on the cross.

The second Sorrowful Mystery is called *The Scourging at the Pillar*. There were some people who did not like Jesus. They did not believe what Jesus taught. They wanted to hurt Jesus so that the people would stop believing in Him. While Jesus was praying in the garden, a group of these people came and took Jesus away. They took Him to the Roman Governor, Pontius Pilate. The people wanted Pilate to put Jesus to death. Pilate thought that if the people saw Jesus punished, they would not want Him to die. Pilate ordered the soldiers to tie Jesus' hands and hurt Him. They hit Jesus with whips. This is called scourging. This whipping hurt Jesus very much.

Those people were very mean to Jesus. Sometimes people are mean to us. We should ask Jesus to help us when people hurt us.

The third Sorrowful Mystery is called *The Crowning with Thorns*. After the men were finished hitting Jesus, they cut branches from a thorn bush. They made a crown out of the branches. They were probably careful not to stick their hands with the sharp thorns. But they did not care about Jesus. They put this crown with its sharp thorns on Jesus' head and pushed it down so that the thorns stuck into Jesus' head. Then they made fun of Jesus and called Him names. Poor Jesus! He suffered all that pain because He loves us.

There are times when people make fun of us or call us names. We should ask Jesus to help us when these things happen to us.

The fourth Sorrowful Mystery is called *The Carrying of the Cross*. The people who did not like Jesus then made a heavy cross out of wood. They gave it to Jesus and made Him carry it a long way to a place called Calvary. Jesus carried the cross willingly, even though it was very heavy. Jesus was so weak after being beaten that He fell down, and the cross fell on top of Him. The people who did not like Jesus were worried that Jesus would not make it to Calvary. So they forced a man named Simon to help Jesus with the heavy cross.

Our difficulties are like crosses, and sometimes they are very heavy for us to carry. But we should remember that Jesus once carried His cross, and that He will help us to carry ours.

The fifth Sorrowful Mystery is called *The Crucifixion*. When Jesus finally made it to the top of the hill of Calvary, the people who did not like Him nailed His hands and feet to the cross. The nails hurt Jesus very much. Instead of being angry, Jesus asked God the Father to forgive the people for what they were doing to Him. When we are hurt by someone, we should try to forgive the person who has hurt us. We should ask Jesus to help us forgive others.

These are the Sorrowful Mysteries of the Rosary. They help us remember all the terrible things that happened to Jesus before He died. If we want to change and become better images of God, we should become followers of Jesus. Our actions should be like His.

Jesus knows how difficult it is for us to act as images of God. When we are in a difficult situation, we can think of the Sorrowful Mysteries. We should ask Jesus to help us make the right choice.

DIFFICULT SITUATIONS

1. **You just found out that you have to move to a new town.**

   How would you feel in this difficult situation?

   How would Jesus choose to act in this situation?

   What should we do as followers of Jesus?

2. **You are having an argument with your best friend.**

   How would you feel in this difficult situation?

   How would Jesus choose to act in this situation?

   What should we do as followers of Jesus?

3. **You received a low grade on your report card.**

   How would you feel in this difficult situation?

   How would Jesus choose to act in this situation?

   What should we do as followers of Jesus?

4. **You are being misunderstood by your parents.**

   How would you feel in this difficult situation?

   How would Jesus choose to act in this situation?

   What should we do as followers of Jesus?

5. **You are being blamed unfairly for something.**

   How would you feel in this difficult situation?

   How would Jesus choose to act in this situation?

   What should we do as followers of Jesus?

DIFFICULT SITUATIONS

After reading the situation, choose the action or actions that you would do as a follower of Jesus. Continue with the others in the same way.

- You find out that some of the things your friend has been telling you are not true. Your friend seems to be lying. What would you do?

  1. Call your friend a liar.

  2. Tell your friend the truth.

  3. Tell your friend how important this friendship is to you.

- Your sister seems to dislike everything you say or do. What would you do?

  1. Ask your sister what she wants you to say or do.

  2. Tell your sister what you like to do.

  3. Get mad at your sister.

- You see someone in your class take an object from the teacher's desk. You know that this is not the first time this has happened. What would you do?

  1. Tell your teacher privately.

  2. Announce what you saw to the class.

  3. Ask the student to return the object.

- You wish that you had everything that your next-door neighbor has—a TV, VCR, and telephone in your bedroom. You are envious of what your neighbor has. What would you do?

  1. Be satisfied with the things you have.

  2. Ask if you could watch TV with your neighbor.

  3. Dislike your neighbor.

DIFFICULT SITUATIONS

- Talk about lazy! You have a friend who will not even talk to you any more because your friend is glued to the couch, watching videos. What would you do?

  1. Talk to your friend.

  2. Stand in front of the TV so that your friend cannot see the videos.

  3. Stop being friends with that person.

- You see your friends being mean to the new person in the class. What would you do?

  1. Tell your teacher privately.

  2. Join your friends in being mean to the new person.

  3. Ask the new person to join you on the playground.

- There is one student in your class who is always goofing off. What would you do?

  1. Talk to the student about it on the playground.

  2. Hit the student.

  3. Have everyone else in the class avoid the student.

- You are having a conversation with some of your friends at recess when another person jumps in and disturbs your group. It seems that this person is always interrupting. What would you do?

  1. Tell the person to be quiet.

  2. Ignore the person.

  3. Remind the person that you are talking and ask the person kindly to wait until you are finished.

DIFFICULT SITUATIONS

- While you are playing a game of kickball, one of the players gets angry and throws a temper tantrum because the team is losing. What would you do?

  1. Politely tell the player either to play ball or to leave.

  2. Help the person understand that winning isn't everything.

  3. Kick the person off the team.

- You and a friend are playing at your house. This friend brags that his toys are better than yours. What would you do?

  1. Ask your friend to bring his toys to your house next time.

  2. Tell your friend to go home.

  3. Don't invite your friend back.

Remember: Jesus is the perfect image of God the Father. The more we think about how Jesus acts and the more we choose to act like Him, the better followers of Him we become and the better images of God we become. Following Jesus can be difficult, but He will help us to act as He acts.

Saint Augustine lived sixteen hundred years ago in what is now Algeria, in North Africa.

When he was a young man, Augustine's heart was filled with disappointment because he could not find happiness. But when he was thirty-two years old, Augustine discovered that following Jesus would make him happy. From then on, Augustine's heart was filled with the desire to serve God and his neighbor. Sometimes it was very difficult for him to fulfill this dream.

Saint Augustine

Augustine was born November 13, 354 A.D., in Tagaste, North Africa. Augustine had an unhappy childhood, and he was often in trouble. He hated school, got into trouble with his friends, and ignored all that his parents told him. The only thing that Augustine cared about was having a good time. He went from one party to another. He also enjoyed playing tricks on people. He told lies, cheated, and stole things.

Even though Augustine hated school, he was good in his studies. Later he began to like school, and he became a teacher and opened his own school in Rome, Italy. For one reason or another, his school was a failure. His students cheated him out of tuition. He was poor, lonely, and often sick.

Augustine continued to have his problems in life. He searched for happiness, but he could not find it. His mother, Monica (who was later declared a saint), never gave up hope. She continued to pray that her son would find happiness in Jesus.

One day in September in the year 386, Augustine found the courage to make the most important decision of his life—to follow Jesus. Finally his life had begun to change for the better. He had found true happiness. He began to live a life of prayer and service. He became a priest and served at one of the churches in his home town. He became the assistant to a local bishop. Soon afterward, the bishop became ill and died, and Augustine became the bishop there. Augustine asked himself, "Why am I a bishop? Why am I in this world?" He answered his questions with, "Only to live as Jesus did."

Augustine continued to pray and to serve God until the day he died. On August 28, 430, at the age of seventy-six, Bishop Augustine quietly died of a fever, praising God.

Augustine was a great teacher, preacher, and pastor. He thought about the actions of Jesus and chose to follow Him. The more Augustine acted like Jesus, the better follower of Jesus he became and the better image of God he became. Even though following Jesus was often difficult for him, he was able to do it with the help of Jesus. Augustine did many things, but it was only in following Jesus that he found real happiness. We celebrate his feast day on August 28.

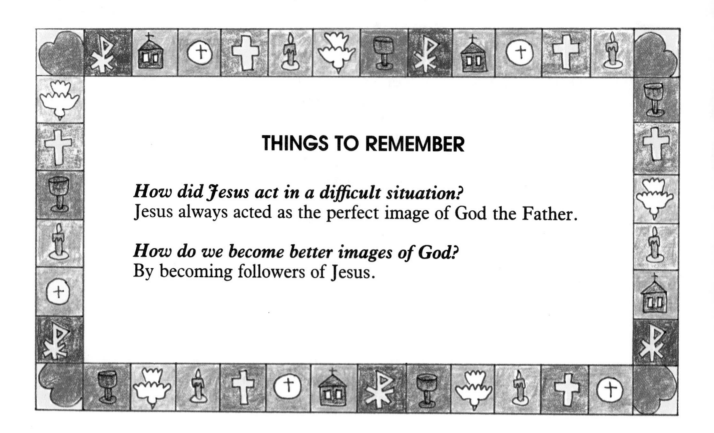

THINGS TO REMEMBER

How did Jesus act in a difficult situation?
Jesus always acted as the perfect image of God the Father.

How do we become better images of God?
By becoming followers of Jesus.

Unit 4
Jesus:
The Perfect Image
of God

13 Jesus Comes to Us

WORDS TO KNOW

Savior: Jesus Christ.
Magi: Wise men.

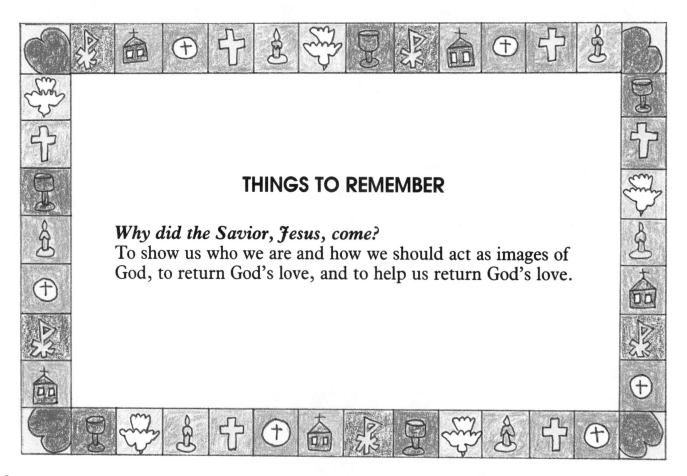

THINGS TO REMEMBER

Why did the Savior, Jesus, come?
To show us who we are and how we should act as images of God, to return God's love, and to help us return God's love.

Jesus, Mary, and Joseph lived like any other family in the town of Nazareth. Joseph was a carpenter, and he taught Jesus how to be a carpenter, too. Jesus went to school, did His chores, and was obedient and respectful to His parents. He enjoyed playing with the other children and was kind and helpful to His neighbors. Most of the people in the town enjoyed His company. Almost no one knew that He was the Savior, God the Son.

Jesus grew in size, strength, and wisdom. He worked as a carpenter until He was about thirty years old. Then Jesus began to teach in parables and to perform miracles.

14   Jesus Does Things for Others

WORDS TO KNOW

miracle: An act that shows the power of God, helps people to have faith in what Jesus taught, and helps them to follow Him.

self-discipline: Watching how we act; changing and improving our actions to act lovingly toward others.

disciples: Followers of Jesus.

drift: Movement caused by the wind.

doubt: Distrust; disbelief.

Original sin damaged our minds, wills, and bodies. Because of original sin, it is difficult for us to know who we are and how we should act. Original sin makes it impossible for us to return the love that God has for us. Jesus came to show us who we are and how we should act as images of God, to return God's love, and to help us return God's love. He did this by teaching, loving, and doing things for people.

Jesus was a terrific teacher. He helped people understand who they are by telling short stories called parables.

His love was the greatest of all loves. He died on the cross to show us how to love, to return the Father's love, and to help us return the Father's love by sharing in God's life.

As God the Son, Jesus could do many things for people that we cannot do. We call these things miracles, because they can be done only by the power of God.

Jesus performed miracles to show us how to act lovingly toward others by what we say and do. He had the power to do many things for Himself. He could have made His life on earth much easier. But He chose to live as we do and to perform His miracles for others.

Jesus used self-discipline. In His miracles He acted lovingly toward others by what He said and did. Jesus used His special powers for others to set an example for all of us.

We should follow the example of Jesus. We cannot perform miracles, but we can use whatever talents and abilities we have to do things for others. We should act lovingly toward others in all that we say and do.

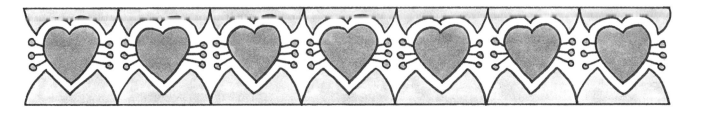

LIVING THE LESSON

1. Because of _____, it is difficult for us to know who we are and how we should act.

2. Original sin damaged our _____, _____, and _____.

3. Original sin made it impossible for us to _____ _____.

4. Jesus came to _____ _____.

5. Jesus shows us how to act lovingly toward others by _____ _____.

6. We can follow the example of Jesus by using our _____ _____ to act lovingly toward others.

Remember, Jesus came to show us who we are and how we should act as images of God, to return God's love, and to help us return God's love. He did this by teaching, loving, and doing things for others. He often showed His love for His disciples (His special followers and friends) by performing miracles.

The disciples followed Jesus almost everywhere. He often performed miracles in front of them.

After witnessing miracles, the disciples knew that Jesus was special, but they found it difficult to imitate Him.

The Calming of the Storm

It was late. Jesus had been teaching all day to a large crowd. He was tired. He asked the disciples to take Him by boat to the other side of the Sea of Galilee so that He could get some rest.

The disciples helped Jesus into the boat and rowed away from the shore. The gentle rocking of the boat caused Jesus to fall asleep. Then, a big storm came up. The disciples were afraid. They didn't know what to do, so they gently shook Jesus to try to wake Him.

Jesus woke up. He said to the sea, "Quiet! Be still!" Suddenly, the wind stopped. Everything was calm.

Then he asked them, "Why are you terrified? Do you not yet have faith?" The disciples were amazed. They wondered who Jesus was that He could make the wind and the sea obey Him.

—Adapted from Mark 4:35–41

In this story, Jesus showed His love for others by calming the storm. By His words and actions, He showed His love for the disciples. We cannot perform miracles, but we can use whatever talents and abilities we have to do things for others. We should act lovingly toward others in all that we say and do.

1. How did Jesus show us who we are and how we should act as images of God, and how did He return God's love and help us return God's love?

   _____

   _____

2. What did Jesus do for other people?

   _____

3. What is a miracle?

   _____

   _____

4. In this story, what miracle did Jesus perform for His disciples?

   _____

The disciples followed Jesus for a long time. They watched Jesus perform many miracles. Finally, after seeing another miracle at sea, the disciples knew that they should follow the example of Jesus. They should act lovingly toward others as Jesus acted lovingly toward them. Let us read about that special miracle now.

Jesus Walks on the Water

One evening, after a long day's work, Jesus wanted to go up on a mountain to pray by Himself. The mountain was close to the sea. Jesus asked His disciples to sail their boat and wait for Him on the other side. Then Jesus went up on the mountain.

When the disciples were a few miles offshore, the wind came up and the boat was being tossed about by the waves. One of the disciples looked up and saw Jesus. The disciple was very frightened. He saw Jesus walking on the water! He told the other disciples to look. They were frightened, too. They thought they were seeing a ghost.

At that moment, Jesus spoke to them. "Take courage; it is I; do not be afraid."

Peter, having doubts, said to Jesus, "If it is you, ask me and I will come to you on the water." Jesus said, "Come."

Peter quickly got out of the boat and walked toward Jesus. Then Peter noticed how strong the wind was, and he became afraid. Peter began to sink. He cried out, "Lord, save me!" Jesus put out His hand and saved Peter from sinking.

—Adapted from Matthew 14:22–33

In this story, Jesus showed his love for others by calming the fears of the disciples and by saving Peter from sinking. We cannot perform miracles, but we can use whatever talents and abilities we have to do things for others. We should act lovingly toward others in all that we say and do.

1. What happened to the disciples?

_____

_____

2. Was Jesus with them?

_____

3. How did Jesus reach the disciples?

_____

_____

4. The disciples were afraid. What did Jesus do?

_____

_____

_____

5. When Peter tried to walk on the water and began to sink, what did Jesus do?

_____

_____

Draw a picture of a loving act that you can do
to show that you are a follower of Jesus.

The Disciples Follow Jesus and Believe

Read all the paragraphs below. Their order is mixed up. In the box in front of each paragraph give the number in which it took place. (For example, put a "1" in front of the first thing that happened.)

	It is evening, and Jesus wants to go up on a mountain to pray. He asks the disciples to sail their boat.
	When Peter has doubts, Jesus saves him from sinking by putting out His hand.
	Jesus tells the disciples to have courage—that it is He they see, not a ghost.
	Peter asks if he can walk to Jesus on the water, and Jesus says to him, "Come."
	The wind comes up, and the boat is tossed about by the waves.
	The disciples see Jesus walking on the water. They are frightened.

Simon Peter knew that Jesus could help his sick mother-in-law. So he went to ask Jesus for that help.

The Cure of Simon's Mother-in-Law

One of Jesus' disciples, Simon, was worried. His mother-in-law was very sick with a fever. He tried everything he could to help her. He decided to ask Jesus for help. Simon, James, and John went to look for Jesus. They found Him working in the temple.

After Jesus had finished His work, He followed the disciples to Simon's house. Jesus walked up to the sick woman and began to speak. The fever left the woman, and she got up and began to wait on Jesus and the disciples.

—Adapted from Luke 4:38–39

In this story, Jesus showed His love for Simon's mother-in-law by curing her. We cannot perform miracles as Jesus did, but we can use whatever talents and abilities we have to do things for others. We should act lovingly toward others in all that we say and do.

LIVING THE LESSON

1. What did Jesus do for other people?

   _____

2. Why did Jesus perform miracles?

   _____

3. How did Jesus show His love for Simon and his mother-in-law?

   _____

Jesus continued to help others by performing miracles. Read the following story about the helpless man near the healing waters of the pool of Bethesda. For thirty-eight years, no one had given him the chance to soak his aching bones. Jesus helped the man by performing a miracle.

The Cure at Bethesda

It was the Sabbath Day. Jesus went up to Jerusalem.

In Jerusalem there was a pool called Bethesda, which was near the entrance of the city. A large number of ill, blind, and crippled people were lying by the pool, hoping to be cured. A man sitting by the pool had been ill for thirty-eight years.

Jesus saw the man and said to him, "Do you want to be well?" The man told Jesus that he wanted to be well, but every time he tried to get to the pool, other people would get there before him. There was never any room left for him.

Jesus said to the man, "Rise, take up your mat, and walk." Immediately the man became well, took up his mat, and walked.
—Adapted from John 5:1–9

In this story, Jesus showed His love for the sick man by curing him. We cannot perform miracles, but we can use whatever talents and abilities we have to do things for others. We should act lovingly toward others in all that we say and do.

LIVING THE LESSON

1. Jesus must have loved the sick man very much. How can you tell?

   _____

2. Why do you think Jesus chose that man? There seemed to be many sick people by the pool.

   _____

   _____

   _____

There was a large crowd following Jesus. More people joined the crowd in every town He visited. The people in the crowd saw how Jesus showed His love for others.

When Jesus did things for others, He showed His love for them. By using His special powers for others, He showed us how to use our own talents and abilities for others, too.

The crowd in the following story saw Jesus perform a wonderful miracle for a poor widow and her son.

The Widow's Son

Jesus was traveling with His disciples to the city of Nain. A large crowd was following them.

As Jesus entered the city, He noticed that a funeral was taking place. A man had died. His body was being taken outside of the city. A woman was following the men who were carrying his body. She was crying. She was the dead man's mother.

When Jesus saw her, He felt sorry for her. He knew that her only son had just died.

He said to her, "Do not weep." Jesus then walked up to her son and touched him. He said to him, "Young man, I tell you, arise!"

The dead man sat up and began to speak, and Jesus gave him to his mother.

—Adapted from Luke 7:11–17

In this story, Jesus showed His love for the widow and her son by bringing the son back to life. We cannot perform miracles as Jesus did, but we can use whatever talents and abilities we have to do things for others. We should act lovingly toward others in all that we say and do.

1. What did Jesus do for the widow?

   _____

2. How did the people know that Jesus loved them?

   _____

3. What do you think the crowd might have done after they saw this miracle?

   _____

   _____

Notice in the following stories how people came to Jesus for help. More and more people were recognizing that Jesus loved them. They could tell that He loved them by what He said and did.

A Woman Who Needed Jesus' Help

In the crowd that was following Jesus there was a sick woman. She had been bleeding inside her body for many years. She spent all of her money visiting many different doctors, and none of them could help her. She had heard about Jesus and was moving through the crowd, trying to get close to Him. She thought that, if she could just touch His clothes, she would be cured.

The woman walked up behind Jesus. She touched His cloak. Suddenly, the bleeding stopped. She had been cured.

Jesus could feel the healing power go out from Him, but He didn't know who had touched Him. He asked the crowd, "Who has touched my clothes?"

The woman fell to her knees before Jesus and told Him the whole story. Jesus told her that she had been cured. She could go in peace and be well again.

Jairus' Daughter

Jesus was on the shore. A large crowd had gathered around Him. A man named Jairus walked up to Jesus. He fell to his knees and said, "My daughter is at the point of death. Please, come lay your hands on her that she may get well and live."

Jesus went off with Jairus to his home. The large crowd followed closely behind.

Meanwhile, a man from Jairus' house came running. He told Jairus that his daughter had died and that it was no longer necessary for Jairus to bring Jesus to the house.

All that Jesus said was, "Do not be afraid."

When they arrived at the house, Jairus took Jesus inside. People were weeping loudly. Jesus said to them, "Why this commotion and weeping? The child is not dead but asleep."

Many of the people there did not believe Jesus. They said mean things to Him. Jesus told them to leave. He took Jairus and his wife into the room where the child was. Jesus took the child's hand in His and said, "Little girl, I say to you, arise!"

The little girl got up and began to walk around. Jesus told the parents to give her something to eat and to say nothing about what had happened.

—Adapted from Mark 5:21–43

In the first story, the bleeding woman touched Jesus' clothes. She felt His great love for her. The bleeding inside her stopped. She had been cured.

In the last story, Jesus went to see Jairus' daughter. Before He got there, she had died. Again, by His words and actions, Jesus showed His great love for others and cured the little girl of her illness.

We cannot perform miracles as Jesus did, but we can use whatever talents and abilities we have to do things for others. We should act lovingly toward others in all that we say and do.

1. What did Jesus do for the woman who needed His help?

   _____

2. Why did Jesus help her?

   _____

3. Jesus helped Jairus' daughter. Why?

   _____

   _____

Jesus and the Children

After Jesus had performed miracles, the crowds that walked with Him were so large that it became impossible for His friends and relatives to get near Him.

People were bringing their children to Jesus to have Him touch them, but the disciples were scolding them for doing so. Jesus said to the disciples, "Let the children come to me; do not prevent them, for the Kingdom of God belongs to such as these. Amen, I say to you, whoever does not accept the Kingdom of God like a child will not enter it." Then Jesus hugged the children, blessed them, and placed His hands upon them.

—Adapted from Mark 10:13–16

In this story, Jesus did not perform a miracle, but He continued to show His love for others. The disciples were afraid that the children would bother Jesus because so many people were around Him all the time. Jesus told them to let the children come to Him. The Kingdom of God belongs to them.

Again, by His words and actions, Jesus showed His love for others. We should use whatever talents and abilities we have to do things for others, too. We should act lovingly toward others in all that we say and do.

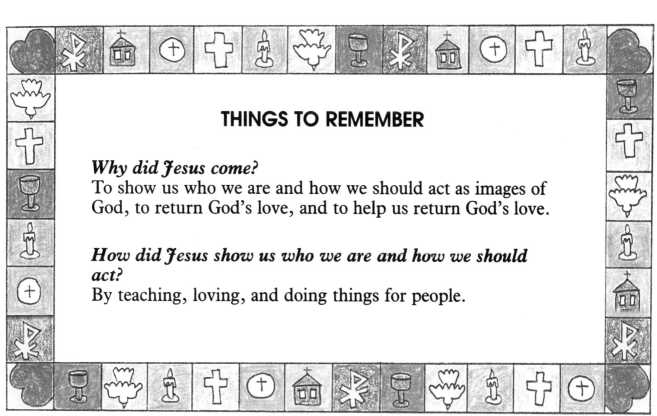

THINGS TO REMEMBER

Why did Jesus come?
To show us who we are and how we should act as images of God, to return God's love, and to help us return God's love.

How did Jesus show us who we are and how we should act?
By teaching, loving, and doing things for people.

Match the description to the miracle.

_____ Jesus said to the sea, "Quiet! Be still!" Suddenly, the wind stopped. Everything was calm.

a. The Widow's Son

_____ The disciples drifted to the middle of the sea. Jesus walked out to meet them.

b. The Cure at Bethesda

_____ For thirty-eight years, the man had tried to be cured. He talked with Jesus and trusted Him. Jesus cured the man.

c. Jairus' Daughter

_____ The sick woman touched Jesus' cloak. Suddenly, she was cured.

d. The Calming of the Storm

_____ Jesus walked up to the sick woman and spoke. Her fever was gone and she got up.

e. Jesus Walks on the Water

_____ Jesus said to the woman's son, "Young man, I tell you, arise!" The man got up and began to speak.

f. A Woman Who Needed Jesus' Help

g. The Cure of Simon's Mother-in-Law

_____ Jesus went inside the little girl's house with her father and mother. He held the child's hand and said, "Little girl, I say to you, arise!"

138

15 Jesus Our Teacher

WORDS TO KNOW

self-discipline: Watching how we act; changing and improving our actions to act lovingly toward others.

miracle: An act that shows the power of God, helps people to have faith in what Jesus taught, and helps them to follow Him.

parable: A short story that teaches a religious lesson.

fig tree: A tree that produces fruits called figs.

barren: Producing little or no fruit.

orchard: A field of fruit trees.

cultivate: To help a plant to grow by loosening the soil around it.

fertilize: To add something to the soil to help a plant to grow.

patient: Willing to wait.

banquet: A fancy meal or dinner party for a large number of people.

humble: Remembering that we are all images of God; that one person is not more important than another.

lame: Weak; having arms or legs that cannot be used normally.

talent: A gift from God; the ability to do something well.

merchant: A buyer or seller of goods for a profit; a storekeeper.

Jesus was a terrific teacher. He helped people understand who they were by telling them short stories called parables.

The parables contained situations that were familiar to the people. When Jesus told these stories, He used everyday experiences of farmers, gardeners, rich people, poor people, travelers, and merchants. Each story always had a special religious message.

Jesus' message is like a light in the dark for us. His message helps lead us to the truth about God and ourselves. By following His message, we also can be a light for others. We can lead others to the truth about God and ourselves.

When we hear a parable, we should do four things:

1. Think about the people in the story and what they did;

2. Look at our own lives and what we do;

3. Think about the truth that Jesus teaches us in the story; and

4. Look again at our own lives and decide whether or not we need to change our way of thinking.

LIVING THE LESSON

1. Original Sin damaged our _____, _____, and _____.

2. Original sin left our minds in the dark. Many times we can't find the _____.

3. Jesus is the _____ and the _____.

4. With the light of Jesus, we can see the _____.
   _____

5. Jesus was a terrific _____.

6. Jesus taught by using short stories called _____.

7. Each story that Jesus told had a special _____.

8. By following the message of Jesus, we can be a _____ for others.

In the following parable, Jesus is telling us that each of us is like a little fig tree. The owner likes the tree very much and watches over it as it grows. Even when the tree does not bear fruit, he does not have it chopped down. He gives it more time to grow.

The Barren Fig Tree

Narrator: A long time ago there was an orchard. It had apple trees (*enter Apple Trees*), banana trees (*enter Banana Trees*), pear trees (*enter Pear Trees*), and one little fig tree (*enter Fig Tree*).

When it was time for the trees to produce fruit, the proud owner walked through his orchard to look at all the fruit on the branches of the various trees. (*Enter the Owner of the orchard.*) Sad to say, the owner found no fruit on his little fig tree. (*Owner sadly bows his head.*) He was disappointed.

(*Enter Gardener.*)

He saw his gardener working in the orchard and asked him to come and look at the little fig tree.

(*Owner waves to Gardener.*)

He said to the gardener:

Owner: For three years I have waited for my fig tree to produce fruit. Since it has not produced any fruit, I want you to chop the tree down.

(*Gardener kneels down and begs.*)

Narrator: The gardener begged the owner:

Gardener: Please leave the tree alone for one more year. I promise to cultivate the ground around it and fertilize it. If the tree still does not produce fruit, then I will chop it down.

Narrator: The owner liked his little fig tree very much. He agreed with the gardener to let it grow one more year.

(The Owner exits. The Gardener stands by the Tree and pretends to rake the soil around it.)

The gardener worked very hard every day to help the fig tree.

(Enter Sun.)

The sun came out to warm the orchard and help the fig tree to grow.

(Enter Cloud and Raindrops. Cloud stands in front of the Sun, while Raindrops walk around the Fig Tree once. Then Cloud and Raindrops sit down.)

Rain came to water the tree.

After nearly a year had passed, the fig tree still did not bear any fruit. The gardener was sad and tired, so he sat down near the tree to rest. *(Gardener sadly sits, and soon he falls asleep.)*

(The Fig Tree turns to show branches bearing fruit. The Owner enters. The Gardener stands, his back to the Tree.)

The gardener stood up when he heard the owner coming toward him. The owner was smiling. The gardener asked:

Gardener: How can you be happy? This is the day that I am to chop down this little fig tree.

(The Owner points to the Tree.)

Narrator: The owner said:

Owner: Cut this wonderful tree down? I couldn't do that! It is the most beautiful tree in my orchard!

(The surprised Gardener turns around to look at the Tree, then happily folds his hands.)

Narrator: The gardener was overjoyed! He folded his hands and thanked God for the wonderful little fig tree.

(Actors put down their props and sit down.)

—Adapted from Luke 13:6–9

We are all images of God. God loves us all very much. He wants us to know this truth about Him and about ourselves.

God the Son became man to teach us the truth. While on earth, Jesus was a very good teacher. He taught people by telling them stories whose religious lesson they could understand.

Each of us is like the fig tree in the parable. God the Father is something like the owner of the little fig tree. The owner liked his tree very much, even though there was no fruit on it. After three years, he was still willing to give the fig tree another chance. He had the gardener—who is like Jesus—cultivate the ground around the tree to help it grow and produce fruit. The tree became very beautiful and did bear fruit.

Sometimes, when we are frustrated, we have a hard time believing that God loves us: schoolwork is hard to do, little brothers and sisters get in the way, big brothers and sisters boss us around, and parents are too tired or busy to help us.

But Jesus tells us the truth. He tells us that we are images of God and that God loves us. So when we stop to clear our minds of those things that frustrate us and think about the truth that Jesus teaches us in the parables, we are reminded that we are images of God and that God loves us very much.

It takes time for us to appreciate this truth. Like the owner of the orchard, God the Father gives us the time that we need to come to an appreciation of this truth. Like the gardener, Jesus helps us to appreciate that we are images of God and that God loves us very much. Once we know this truth, then we, like the fig tree, can produce fruit by sharing this truth with others.

All of us are rich in so many different ways. We are healthy or we are skillful in sports, reading, math, spelling, mowing the lawn, or collecting baseball cards! What we know, or have, or can do should be shared. When we share our thoughts, our goods, and our talents, we are sharing our love. We are following the teaching of Jesus that God loves every person and that we should love others as He loves them.

Everyone should follow the teaching of Jesus and treat others as they should be treated, as images of God. Some people do not treat others as images of God. They do not believe the truth that God loves us and that we should love others as God loves us.

In the following parable, the rich man did not believe the truth that each person is an image of God and is loved by God. He did not think that he should love other persons as God loves them. He did not treat them fairly.

The Rich Man and Lazarus

There was a rich man whose everyday meals were a feast! He dressed up in fancy clothes for every meal. His table was covered with fine tablecloths and dishes. His servants waited on him and brought him delicious meals.

Every day, while the rich man was eating, a poor man named Lazarus sat on the rich man's doorstep, hoping for some table scraps. Lazarus was given some leftovers of food, but he was never invited inside for a good meal.

When the poor man died, he was taken to heaven, because he knew the truth, believed the truth, and showed others that he believed the truth. When the rich man died, he did not go to heaven. He had had many good things in his life, but he had not shared them.

The rich man did not remember Jesus' teaching that everyone is an image of God, that God loves us, and that we should love others as God loves us.

—Adapted from Luke 16:19–25

Lazarus was an image of God, and he tried to live as an image of God. Lazarus knew the truth, believed the truth, and showed others that he believed the truth. We should be like him.

We should not be like the rich man. We should remember the teaching of Jesus that everyone is an image of God and is loved by God. We should love everyone as God does. We want to follow the teaching of Jesus.

Mother Teresa (of Calcutta) follows the teaching of Jesus by treating others as images of God. She believes that God loves each person and that we should love others as He loves them and us. By her life she has shown that she believes this truth: she shares her love by helping others in any way she can.

Mother Teresa of Calcutta

As a young woman, Mother Teresa lived in India as a member of the Loretto nuns. She dedicated her life entirely to God. She chose to do so because she knew that God loved her. She wished to show her love in return. But, as she prayed and worked with the Loretto nuns, she knew in her heart that she was not sharing all of the love she had to give.

So one day she left the Loretto nuns. She was determined to "walk with God". As God's image, she wished to share His love where she was most needed—with the poorest of the poor.

She had only five rupees in her pocket, which is about the same as five dollars. Where could she go with so little money?

A person cannot buy very much with five dollars. Mother Teresa knew that. She decided that, because she was going to work with the poor people, she was going to live with them, too.

Mother Teresa went to the slums of Calcutta. Slums are parts of large cities. The very poorest people live in the slums. They have very few jobs, the buildings are in very poor condition, and there is a shortage of running water. In the slums, almost everything and everyone is dirty, and many people are sick because they do not have enough to eat or water to clean themselves with.

It hurt Mother Teresa to see so many people sad and in pain. Many of them were starving, diseased, or sick. She began to help by finding water for the people and by nursing the sores of those who had diseases. She cooked rice for the starving, so that they would have at least one meal a day.

The people saw that Mother Teresa loved them, and her efforts to help them made them feel better. They shared their love with her as she shared her love with them. She knew and lived the truth that Jesus taught: God loves every person very much, and, as images of God, we should love God in return. We should treat everyone as an image of God and love others as God loves them.

Mother Teresa knew that the poor people of the slums needed a place to go for help. She knew also that she herself could not reach everyone who needed her care. She decided to find others who would be willing to share their love as she did. She talked to others and asked for their help. Soon many others came to help her. She was able to start a new religious group of people who dedicated themselves to helping the neediest. This group is called the Missionaries of Charity.

Missionaries are persons who dedicate themselves to a religious life so that they can go to other countries (or to other parts of their own country) to love and serve God by helping others. Helping others "for charity" means helping them for the love of God.

The people who joined Mother Teresa's Missionaries of Charity included men and women who came from all over the world to spend their lives helping the poor.

With the gifts of money, food, and supplies they received from others, the Missionaries of Charity started homes where abandoned children could live and where the dying could be cared for. They set up medical clinics staffed by doctors and nurses to care for the sick. They set up food stations and cooked large pots of rice to feed the hungry. The Missionaries of Charity have done much to improve the lives of people living in the slums.

Mother Teresa and her Missionaries of Charity know the truth: we should treat others as images of God. They know that God loves every person and that we should love others as God does. They believe these truths and they show others that they believe by loving them as images of God.

So many times, we want to be first in everything—first in line, first one up to bat, first one to finish schoolwork. But first is not always best. Trying to be first can sometimes cause us to think mean thoughts, or to make wrong choices, or to act in an unkind way.

In the parable that follows, the truth that Jesus teaches us is that as images of God we should be humble. To be humble is to remember that we are *all* images of God. One person is not more important than another. We should not try to be first in order to make ourselves seem more important than others.

We should respect the dignity of other people. If you do your best on a test and receive an "A", while someone else does her best on the same test and receives a "C", do not brag about your grade. Instead, praise the other person for trying her best. We cannot all be good at everything.

The Lowest Seat

Jesus went to a wedding banquet. He was watching people choose where they were going to sit at the long table. He told His followers that, when they are invited to a special banquet, they should not choose to sit in the places of honor. Other guests may have been chosen to sit there. Then the host would have to ask those who had chosen to sit in the places of honor to move to the seats farther down the table, so that the other guests could sit in the places of honor. It would be quite embarrassing to have to move to a lower place.

Jesus suggested to His followers that they choose to go to the lower seats first. Then it might happen that the host will come to them and invite them to sit at a higher place. "For everyone who exalts himself will be humbled, but the one who humbles himself will be exalted."

Then Jesus suggested that, next time, the host should invite to his banquet the poor, the crippled, the blind, and the lame, instead of inviting relatives and friends.

These needy people probably would not be able to invite him for a feast in return. But the host would be blessed indeed. He would be acting as an image of God. He would be treating everyone, especially those in need, as images of God. He would be recognizing that the poor are important persons, too.

—Adapted from Luke 14:7–14

Everyone has talents. Talents are gifts from God. They are the abilities that help us do certain things well. We should thank God every day for the abilities we have, rather than complain about abilities we don't have.

We also should *use* our talents. If talents are not used, they become like a bicycle left outdoors in the rain and the cold. If a bicycle is not used and not kept in a dry, protected place, it becomes rusty and difficult to ride. In the same way, if we don't use our talents, they can become very hard for us to use.

When something is very hard for us to do, we are tempted to stop thinking about it, to stop choosing to do it, and to act in a lazy way by taking an easy way out.

Jesus reminds us in the following parable that our talents are special. If we use our talents, they make us stronger persons, bring joy to ourselves and to others, and are a help to others. We should be thankful for our abilities and not let our talents get "rusty".

The Silver Pieces

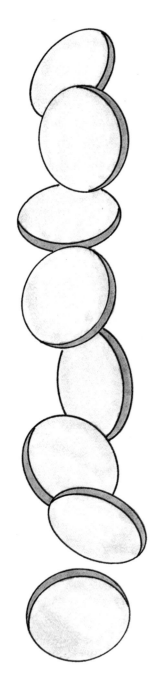

(*A man is standing by a table with his suitcase on the floor. There is money on the table.*)

A man was going on a long trip. He wanted to make sure that everything he owned was taken care of, including his money. So, before he left, he called his servants to his office.

(*The man gestures with his hand. Three servants enter.*)

"I am going on a long trip", he told his servants. "I want each of you to take care of my money while I am away."

(*The servants look surprised as the man hands each of them a part of his money.*)

He gave each of the servants silver pieces to take care of. He made sure that each person could manage the amount of money that he was given. "Remember," he said to them, "I am trusting you with the money I have given you. Use it as I would use it."

(*The master exits, carrying his suitcase. The servants exit. After a moment, the first servant and a landowner enter. They look at a map. The first servant gives the landowner five silver coins. He then shows the audience a picture of the land he has just purchased. The landowner exits.*)

The first servant received from his master five silver coins. He traded the five coins for a parcel of land. And then he sold the land for twice the amount he had paid for it.

(Enter a buyer, who wishes to buy the land. The first servant holds up a price tag for twice the amount he had paid for it. The buyer gives the servant ten silver coins. The servant smiles and shows the audience a picture of the land with a "Sold" sign across it. The servant and the buyer exit.)

(The second servant and an artist, carrying a painting, enter. The artist shows the painting to the servant. The servant gives the artist two silver coins, and the artist hands him the painting. The artist exits.)

The second servant received two silver pieces. He traded the money for a painting, and then sold it for twice the amount he had paid for it.

(Enter the buyer, who wishes to buy the painting. He gives the servant four silver coins for the painting. They shake hands and exit. The third servant enters and begins digging near the foot of a tree.)

But the third servant, who received one piece of silver, went off and dug a hole in the ground and buried his master's money because he was too lazy to try to put it to good use.

(The servant places the silver coin in the ground, buries it, and exits. The master returns, puts his suitcase down, and summons his three servants.)

Finally, the master returned home from his journey. He called his servants to his side and said to them: "So, tell me, my faithful servants, what have you done with my money?"

(The first servant steps forward and proudly hands his master ten silver coins.)

The first servant presented his master with the ten pieces of silver. With pride he said, "I bought land with your money. When the value of the land went up, I sold the land and got twice as much money as I had paid for it."

(The first servant steps back. The master smiles. The second servant steps forward.)

The second servant came forward and handed his master four silver coins. Happily, he explained, "I bought a painting for the two pieces of silver you gave me. Later, I met a buyer who wanted the painting and willingly paid me twice the amount I had paid for it."

(The master smiles again, as the second servant steps back. The third servant comes before his master, his head hung low.)

The servant who had received one silver piece stepped forward slowly. He knew that his master would not praise what he had done. He said to his master: "I was too lazy to try to do anything with the silver coin you gave me, so I buried it in the ground. Here it is."

(The third servant hands his master one silver coin and steps back. The master shakes his head.)

The master said to the third servant: "I am very disappointed in you. I would not have given you the money if I hadn't thought you could handle it well. Joy comes from using what you are given, not from burying it in the ground. Because you did not use the money I gave you, you will lose it."

(The master exits. The first and second servants follow happily after him. The third servant exits sadly.)

—Adapted from Matthew 25:14–29

In this parable, the truth that Jesus is teaching us is that we should use the talents God has given each of us, and use them as well as the first two servants used the money their master had given them. God knows how much each person can handle. He doesn't frustrate us by expecting too little or too much from us. He expects us to use our talents. We frustrate ourselves when we don't use the talents we have been given or when we try to do things that are beyond our ability.

The master was equally happy with the two servants who used their talents. God is happy, too, when we use whatever talents we have. Remember the truth that Jesus teaches us: use the talents you have been given!

Write one talent on each of the "coins".
Then cut out the coins.

Write your name on
the back of each coin.

Treasures are great! They can make us happy. Sometimes we have to search very hard to find them.

The Kingdom of God is the greatest treasure that we can find. God's Kingdom includes everyone who acts as an image of God and shares God's life.

Every day, we find clues that lead us to the treasure. Some of the clues are in the parables of Jesus, which teach us about God and ourselves.

The parables teach us that we are images of God, that God loves us very much, and that we should love others as God loves them and us. The parables also teach us to be humble and to use our talents wisely.

The more people there are who listen to the parables and act as God's images, the more people there will be in God's Kingdom. Jesus tells us about God's Kingdom in the following parables.

The Treasure and the Pearl

The Kingdom of God is like a treasure buried in a field. A man finds it. He is so excited that he hides it just to be able to dig it up and find it again. The treasure gives him so much joy that he sells everything he has and buys that field.

The Kingdom of God is also like a merchant searching for fine pearls. While searching, he finds a perfect pearl worth a lot of money. He wants that pearl more than anything else in the whole world. So he sells everything he has so that he can buy it.

—Adapted from Matthew 13:44–46

We are looking for God's Kingdom. We are just like the man hunting for treasure or the merchant searching for pearls. The treasure represents everyone who acts as an image of God and shares God's life both here on earth and in heaven. The perfect pearl represents the same thing as the treasure.

We should be like the man who found the treasure and like the man who found the perfect pearl in the parables. If we are not following the teaching of Jesus in some way, we should "sell" our old way of life and choose to follow the teachings of Jesus. It is not always easy to make such a change.

In these two stories, Jesus presents us with the truth that the Kingdom of God is worth every effort to find it and be part of it.

The more people there are who act as images of God and share God's life, the larger the Kingdom of God will be. By following the teaching of Jesus, we can do our part to increase the Kingdom of God. The Kingdom of God is going to be much larger than we can ever imagine.

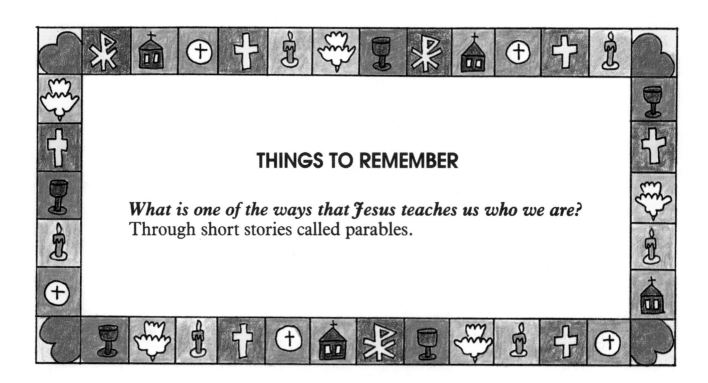

THINGS TO REMEMBER

What is one of the ways that Jesus teaches us who we are?
Through short stories called parables.

156

16 Jesus Returns God's Love

WORDS TO KNOW

betray: To do something against a person who trusts you.

As Jesus was walking with His disciples one day, He told them that
He was going to suffer greatly. He told them that He would be
killed, but that after three days He would rise from the dead. By
telling His disciples this, He was preparing them for His death and
Resurrection. Jesus died on the cross to show us how to act, to
return God the Father's love, and to help us to return God's love.
—Adapted from Mark 8:31

Some people did not believe in Jesus and did not follow Him. They wanted to arrest Him and kill Him. But they had to find someone who would help them have Jesus arrested.

One of the Apostles, Judas Iscariot, was willing to help. Those who wanted Jesus arrested promised to give Judas money for his help. Judas promised to find a time to have Jesus arrested.

The Passover was coming soon. The Passover is celebrated each year by the Jewish people to thank God for freeing them from the Egyptians. Judas thought he might find a time to have Jesus arrested during this celebration.

The disciples asked Jesus, "Where do you want us to go and prepare for you to eat the Passover?" Jesus said, "Go into the city and a man will meet you, carrying a jar of water. Follow him. Wherever he enters, say to the master of the house, 'The Teacher says, "Where is my guest room where I may eat the Passover with my disciples?"' Then he will show you a large upper room furnished and ready. Make the preparations for us there."

The disciples went off. When they reached the city, everything happened just as Jesus had told them. They prepared the Passover supper.

When evening came, Jesus entered the room with the twelve Apostles. They sat down at the table and prepared to eat. Jesus said, "I say to you, one of you will betray me, one who is eating with me." One by one, the Apostles said, "Surely, not I!"

Later, while they were all eating, Jesus took bread and said the blessing, broke it, and gave it to them, and said, "Take it; this is my body." Then he took a cup, gave thanks, and gave it to them, and they all drank from it. He said to them, "This is my blood of the covenant, which will be shed for many."

This special meal that Jesus shared with the Apostles is called the Last Supper. It was the first Mass.

—Adapted from Mark 14:1–4; 10–25

Jesus was about to suffer many terrible things. But Jesus willingly accepted all His sufferings and offered His sufferings to God the Father to save us from our sins. By doing so, He shows us how we should act, He returned the Father's love, and He helps us to return God's love.

After the Last Supper, Jesus was betrayed by Judas, one of His disciples.

Then Jesus was arrested and led away. Some soldiers beat Jesus and made fun of Him. Jesus was then given a large wooden cross to carry. He had to carry the cross to a place outside the city. When Jesus got to the place, called Calvary, the soldiers nailed Jesus to the cross. Jesus prayed that His Father would forgive the soldiers. Then Jesus died.

Some women came to the tomb where the body of Jesus was buried. They brought spices that they had prepared. They expected to find a huge stone covering the entrance to Jesus' tomb. But when they arrived at the tomb, they found the stone at the entrance of the tomb had been rolled back. When they entered the tomb, they found that Jesus' body was gone. They wondered what had happened to Jesus. While they were standing there, two men in dazzling white garments appeared. They asked, "Why do you seek the living one among the dead? He is not here, but he has been raised. Remember what he said to you while he was still in Galilee, that the Son of Man must be handed over to sinners and be crucified, and rise on the third day." When they heard this, the women remembered Jesus' words.

As the women left the tomb, they met the Apostles. The women told the Apostles what had happened to them. It seemed so fantastic that the Apostles refused to believe them. Peter, however, ran to the tomb. He bent down and saw nothing but the linens that had been used to wrap Jesus' body. Peter left in amazement.

—Adapted from Luke 24:1–12

Jesus' death on the cross was the greatest act of love ever. By dying on the cross, Jesus showed us how to act. He showed us that we are to love God and others. By dying on the cross, Jesus also returned God's love and helps us to return God's love. By His death on the cross, Jesus restored the friendship between God and us, and He made it possible for us to share God's life. With God's life, we are able to return God's love.

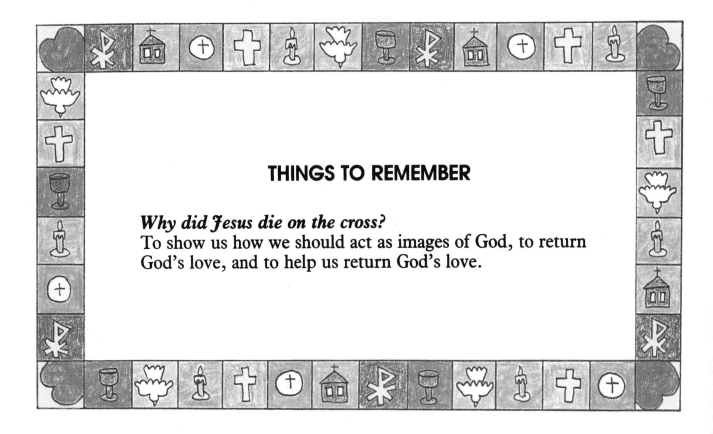

THINGS TO REMEMBER

Why did Jesus die on the cross?
To show us how we should act as images of God, to return God's love, and to help us return God's love.

Unit 5
The Church:
The Person of Christ

17 Mary

WORDS TO KNOW

Immaculate Conception: From the very first moment of Mary's life, she was without original sin.

Annunciation: The visit of the angel Gabriel to Mary, asking her to be the Mother of Jesus.

THINGS TO REMEMBER

How did Mary become the Mother of Jesus?
Through the power of the Holy Spirit.

A very long time ago, God the Father chose to send His Son, Jesus, to live with us on earth. Jesus would show us who we are and how we should act. He would return God's love and help us to return God's love.

According to Tradition, living in the town of Nazareth was an elderly couple named Ann and Joachim. They had prayed for years to God, asking Him to send them a child. God gave them a daughter, whom they named Mary.

From the very first moment of her life, even before she was born, Mary was without original sin. In other words, from the very first moment of her life, Mary shared God's life, grace. This special privilege given to Mary by God is called her "Immaculate Conception". She was given this gift because she was to be the Mother of Jesus.

The Annunciation, the Visitation, and the Nativity

One day, God the Father sent a messenger, the angel Gabriel, to the house where Mary lived. The angel said, "Hail, favored one! The Lord is with you." Mary was afraid. She did not understand the angel's greeting and wondered what it meant. Then the angel said to her, "Do not be afraid, Mary, for you have found favor with God." The angel went on to explain to Mary that God was asking her to be the mother of a son and to name the baby Jesus. He would be the Savior. Mary did not understand and asked how she could be a mother. The angel told her that it would happen through the power of the Holy Spirit, and that nothing is impossible for God. Mary said, "Behold, I am the handmaid of the Lord. May it be done to me according to your word." With this answer, Mary was saying that she would do whatever God asked. We call this the Annunciation.

The angel told Mary that her cousin Elizabeth was going to have a baby, too. Then the angel left her. After the angel left, Mary decided to go to visit Elizabeth and to share all the good news. We call the visit of Mary to Elizabeth the Visitation.

—Adapted from Luke 1:26–38

After Mary returned home from visiting Elizabeth, Mary and Joseph were married. Then they found out that they had to travel to the town of Bethlehem to be counted in a census. We all know what happened when Mary and Joseph reached Bethlehem. Jesus was born! We call Jesus' birth the Nativity.

Jesus loved His Mother very much, and Mary loved Jesus. Because Mary loved Jesus so much, she stayed near Him during all His suffering. When Jesus was crucified, Mary stood at the foot of the cross with the Apostle John. Jesus said to His Mother, "Woman, behold, your son." Then Jesus spoke to John. "Behold, your mother" (John 19:26–27). In this way Jesus made Mary our Mother.

Jesus loved Mary so much that He did a very special thing for her. When Mary's life on earth was over, Jesus brought Mary, body and soul, to reign with Him forever in heaven. We call this event the Assumption of Mary. Mary is our Mother in heaven, and she helps us by her prayers. We should honor and love Mary.

The Church celebrates many feast days for Mary.

The Church celebrates many feast days for Mary.

January 1	Mary as the Mother of God (Mary's "Mother's Day")
March 25	The Annunciation
May 31	The Visitation
August 15	The Assumption
August 22	The Queenship of Mary
September 8	Mary's Birthday
September 15	Mary as Our Lady of Sorrows (remembering the suffering Mary endured)
October 7	Mary as Our Lady of the Rosary
November 21	The Presentation of Mary
December 8	The Immaculate Conception
December 12	Mary as Our Lady of Guadalupe

Mary is the Queen of heaven and earth. She is our Mother in heaven. She helps us by her prayers. In return, we should pray to her for her help. One way we can honor Mary is by praying the Rosary. Mary gave us the Rosary to help us pray and bring us closer to Jesus. By praying the Rosary, we love and honor Mary, our Mother.

WORDS TO KNOW

miracle: An act that shows the power of God; it helps people have faith in what Jesus taught and to follow Him.

self-discipline: Watching how we act; changing and improving our actions to act lovingly toward others.

communion of persons: A group of two or more persons who work together, love each other, and help each other love as God loves.

diocese: The people and the parishes under the care of a bishop.

parish: A local church community.

universal Church: The Church throughout the world; all the people from all the dioceses continuing the work of Jesus together.

foreman: A leader of a group of workers.

When Jesus was on earth, He taught people the truth about God the Father. He also taught them the truth about who they were and how they should act. One of the ways He did this was through the parables.

Out of love for God the Father and all of us, Jesus died on the cross. By loving God the Father and others, He showed us how to love. Also, by dying on the cross, Jesus returned God's love. Through His death on the cross, Jesus gives us the strength to love God, too. Jesus has risen and is now in heaven. But Jesus did not abandon us. He left us the sacraments. The sacraments are physical signs, given to us by Jesus, through which Jesus meets us and gives us His grace.

Jesus used self-discipline. He had the power to do many things for Himself. He could have made His life on earth much easier. Instead, He chose to live His life as we do and to perform miracles for others. He used His special powers for others to show us how to use our talents to benefit others.

Jesus commanded the Apostles to teach all people the things that He had taught them through the parables, to help all people celebrate the sacraments and receive God's life, and to show all people how to use their talents to benefit others.

Jesus Asks Peter a Question

One day, after the Resurrection of Jesus, Peter, one of the Apostles, decided to go fishing. Some of the other Apostles thought it was a great idea and asked Peter if they could join him.

After fishing all night, they had caught nothing. They were very disappointed. There was a man standing on the shore, watching them.

The Apostles did not know that it was Jesus standing on the shore, watching them. He asked them, "Children, have you caught anything to eat?" They answered, "No."

Jesus then told them to cast the net over the other side of the boat. The Apostles did what Jesus told them to do. They caught so many fish that they could not pull the net in! Then they knew that the man on the shore was Jesus.

Jesus said to them, "Come, have breakfast." After breakfast, Jesus asked Simon Peter, "Simon, son of John, do you love me?" Peter answered, "Yes, Lord, you know that I love you." Jesus said to Peter, "Feed my lambs." Then Jesus asked Peter again, "Simon, son of John, do you love me?" Peter again answered, "Yes, Lord, you know that I love you." Jesus replied, "Tend my sheep." He asked Peter a third time, "Simon, son of John, do you love me?" Peter was disappointed that Jesus had to ask a *third* time, so he said to Jesus, "Lord, you know everything; you know that I love you." Jesus said to Peter, "Feed my sheep."

—Adapted from John 21:1–17

This story shows how Jesus asked Peter to teach people the things that Jesus had taught him through the parables, to help all people celebrate the sacraments and receive God's life, and to show all people how to use their talents to benefit others.

Jesus asked all His Apostles to carry on His work in a special way. Jesus blessed the Apostles and told them that He would send the Holy Spirit to help guide them.

Jesus Visits the Apostles

A short time after Jesus had risen from the dead, the Apostles met in a locked room. They missed Jesus very much. They needed to talk to each other and comfort each other. They were talking about what Jesus had told them. Jesus had told them that He loved them and that He would always be with them.

While they were still talking, Jesus suddenly appeared before them! He "stood in their midst and said to them, 'Peace be with you.'"

When Jesus had said this, He showed them the wounds in His hands and His side. The Apostles rejoiced when they recognized Jesus!

"Jesus said to them again, 'Peace be with you. As the Father has sent me, so I send you.'" By saying that He was sending His Apostles, Jesus was asking them to teach all people the things that He had taught them through the parables, to help all people celebrate the sacraments and receive God's life, and to show all people how to use their talents to benefit others. And when Jesus had said this, He breathed on them and said to them, "Receive the Holy Spirit."

—Adapted from Luke 24:36; John 20:19–23

The power of the Holy Spirit is stronger than we can ever imagine! The Apostle Paul could feel the Holy Spirit's power in him. Especially when it was hard to teach what Jesus taught, Paul knew the Holy Spirit was there, guiding him.

Not all people wanted to listen to Paul. Some people even put him in prison! But Paul did not give up. His courage was still strong.

While in prison, he wrote a letter to his friend Timothy.

Paul's Letter

Paul wrote that he was very grateful to God for everything that God had given him. Paul also wrote that he could hardly wait to see Timothy again.

Paul reminded Timothy that his grandmother and his mother had great faith in Jesus. Paul believed that their faith lived in his good friend, too.

So Paul told Timothy not to worry about him, a prisoner for the Lord. Instead, Paul recalled how he had blessed Timothy and made him a bishop. As a bishop, Timothy would teach all people the things that Jesus had taught him through the parables, help all people celebrate the sacraments and receive God's life, and show all people how to use their talents to benefit others.

—Adapted from 2 Timothy 1:1–8

Besides Timothy, the Apostles blessed other men so that they too could teach all people the things that Jesus had taught them through the parables, help all people celebrate the sacraments and receive God's life, and show all people how to use their talents to benefit others. Together, these men, along with the other baptized, were the first members of the Church. Today, we have the bishops and the Pope to teach us the things that Jesus taught through the parables, to help us celebrate the sacraments and receive God's life, and to show us how to use our talents to benefit others.

It is all the baptized members of the Church working together— including deacons, priests, bishops, and the Pope—who make up the Church, God's family.

God's family is very large. It includes Christian people all over the world. It includes our immediate family, our parish, the diocese, and the Catholic people all over the world. Together, all the Catholic people form the universal Church.

As members of the Church, we are to do all that we can to continue Jesus' mission of bringing the "Good News of Salvation" to all the world. As members of the Church, we should follow the Pope and the bishops. The Pope and the bishops teach all people what Jesus taught them through the parables, they help all people celebrate the sacraments and receive God's life, and they show all people how to use their talents to benefit others. By following the Pope and the bishops, we find out who we are and how we should act, we receive God's life in the sacraments, and we come to know how to use our talents to benefit others.

Pretend that you are a reporter for Christ. As a reporter, it is your job to spread the "Good News". Before you can spread the Good News, you have to look at what Jesus taught us. Think about your favorite parable. Think about the people in the story and what they did. Look at what people do today. Then think about the truth that Jesus teaches us in that parable and how that truth applies to us today. Retell the story in your own words on the next page.

THE DAILY
SONSHINE

At Mass, during the Gospel, we hear the parables that Jesus taught. The parables tell us the truth about God the Father and ourselves. Priests and teachers help us understand the truth.

We need to share the truth with the members of our family. Reading the Bible, praying together, and discussing what we have learned are ways we can better understand who we are.

Jesus showed His great love by dying on the cross. We can show our love for God the Father by receiving the sacraments and reminding the other members of our family to receive the sacraments, too.

Jesus served others by performing miracles. We can serve others by using our talents; even to help our brothers and sisters when we don't feel like it.

When we gather together as a parish community, we form a much larger family. There are more people helping each other.

Teachers, priests, and other members of the Church can help explain parables that we do not understand. Sacraments are times of great celebration. Together, the parish community can feel the excitement and joy of receiving God's life.

Some families are poor and cannot help themselves. These families need the help of the *parish family*. Members of the parish can put their talents together to help people in need.

The churches in our diocese and all of the Catholic people all over the world form the universal Church. *Together* we can help each other to understand the truth within the parables, to receive the sacraments, and to use our talents to serve others. Whether in the family, the parish, the diocese, or the universal Church, we do all of these things by following our leaders, the Pope and the bishops. They teach all people the things that Jesus taught them through the parables, help all people celebrate the sacraments and receive God's life, and show all people how to use their talents to benefit others.

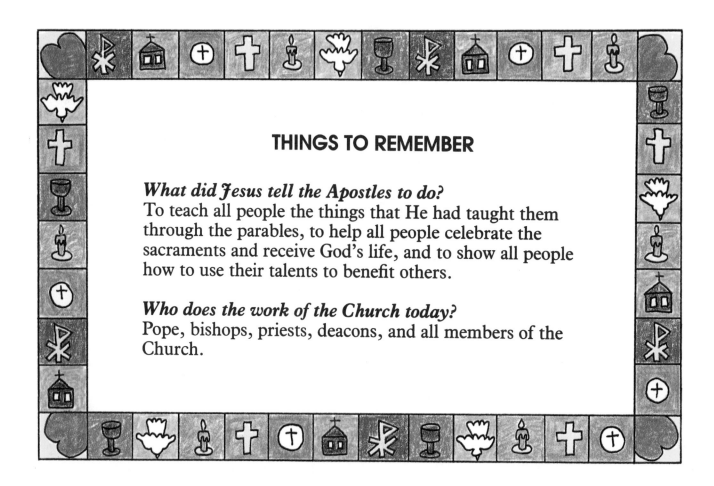

THINGS TO REMEMBER

What did Jesus tell the Apostles to do?
To teach all people the things that He had taught them through the parables, to help all people celebrate the sacraments and receive God's life, and to show all people how to use their talents to benefit others.

Who does the work of the Church today?
Pope, bishops, priests, deacons, and all members of the Church.

My Family

My Church

Bishop

Pope

181

19 Serving Others in the Church Community

WORDS TO KNOW

parish: A local church community.
diocese: The people and the parishes under the care of a bishop.

To have a successful
church community as the Apostles
did, we must first begin with our own families.
Each family is a small community all by itself. Family members
should pray, receive the sacraments, and serve others together.

Serving everyone within our family sounds like a big job. But Jesus
does not expect us to try to take care of all problems and needs
right away by ourselves. He just wants us to use our own talents
and help a little bit at a time. Even helping someone smile can be a
big help.

This prayer reminds us to do *what* we can *when* we can, and to get
help with the rest:

> **God, grant me the serenity [peaceful ability]**
> **to accept the things I cannot change,**
> **courage to change the things I can,**
> **and wisdom to know the difference.**

We have talents that are helpful to every member of our families!
Of course, there are things that we cannot do, but there are *many*
things that we *can* do to meet the physical and material needs of
others. We need only the courage and the patience to try them.

LIVING THE LESSON

1. How can we "look at the world through the very eyes of Christ"?

_____

_____

_____

2. Where do we begin to help others?

_____

_____

_____

3. How do we serve others within our own families?

_____

_____

_____

4. Think about the things that you do to help meet the physical and material needs of the members of your family and write them down.

_____

_____

_____

_____

_____

_____

Jesus was always looking for ways to benefit others by using His powers to take care of their physical and material needs. Pope John Paul II said, "The Church looks at the world through the very eyes of Christ."

Because all baptized Catholics are members of the Church, *we* should look at the *world* the way that Jesus did. We should look for ways to help people *everywhere* and then use our talents to benefit others by meeting their physical and material needs.

Caring for the members of our own family community is a good place to start. But we belong to more than one community, and there are many people outside our family who need our help and support, too.

The next place to look for ways to serve others is within our own local church community. Our local church community or parish helps others both inside the church building and out!

When we go to Mass, we see many people volunteering their time and talents to make sure that everything necessary for the celebration of Mass is prepared.

Health, food, and friendship are three things that people need. When people are sick or dying, they often need to be shown that other people care. Many parishes have members who will visit the sick at home or in the hospital. Parishes also have groups of people with the same health problems who meet together for support. They also have groups for concerned family members of those who are ill.

Many people are hungry and cannot afford a weekly trip to the grocery store. Church members donate food and place it on shelves in a special place. Needy people can go to the "Food Shelves" and select what they need for their families.

Some people cannot walk or drive to local "Food Shelves". Volunteer drivers for "Meals on Wheels" bring the food to the needy.

Friends help us to enjoy life. Your parish can help you see friends more often or meet new people if you are lonely.

Many parishes have a social hour after one of the Masses that includes coffee, doughnuts, and juice. It's a great time to relax and enjoy each other's company.

Other social groups and events in a parish might include: a festival, a home and school association, an usher's club, a senior citizen's group, a women's club, a youth group, a young adults' club, a Cub Scout pack, a Boy Scout troop, and a Campfire group. With such a list, there are many to choose from!

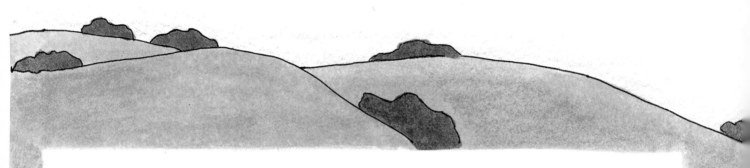

While Jesus was on earth, He helped many people by performing miracles. The following story gives one example.

Jesus Feeds a Crowd

One day, Jesus quietly took the Apostles to a town called Bethsaida. He wanted to meet with them privately, away from the crowds that had been following Him.

The crowds, however, heard about the meeting and followed Jesus anyway. Jesus accepted their company. He spoke to them about the Kingdom of God and healed those who needed to be cured.

As nighttime approached, the Apostles became worried. There were about five thousand people following Jesus. All of them needed food to eat and a place to sleep. The Apostles went to Jesus and said, "Dismiss the crowd so that they can go to surrounding villages and farms and find lodging and provisions."

Jesus said to the Apostles, "Give them some food yourselves."

They replied, "Five loaves and two fish are all we have, unless we ourselves go and buy food for all these people."

Jesus told the Apostles to ask the people to sit in groups of about fifty. Then He took the loaves and fish, blessed them, broke them, and gave them to the Apostles to pass out to the large crowd.

The people ate until they were full. When the leftovers were picked up, they filled twelve baskets.

—Adapted from Luke 9:10–17

Today, Jesus has many followers in families, parishes, dioceses, and the whole world. He wants all of these people to be fed and clothed and to have shelter, too.

Our local parish community tries very hard to help people who need food, clothing, and shelter. But sometimes the parish does not know how to answer certain questions or how to solve certain problems. Sometimes there isn't enough food, clothing, shelter, time, or money for the needy. The priest or parishioners can then turn to the diocese for help. A diocese is the people and the parishes under the care of a bishop.

Bishops primarily teach all people what Jesus taught through the parables. But bishops also put the efforts of many people together to help others in need of guidance, food, clothing, and shelter.

The bishop is like a shepherd, and we are the sheep of his flock. The shepherd meets the physical and materials needs of the sheep. The bishop meets the physical and material needs of the people.

The bishop of a diocese has many talented people working for him. These people have volunteers who are available to help anyone from any of the parishes in that diocese.

The Pope, a very special bishop, is the leader of the universal Church. He helps to bring the "Good News" to all the people of the world by meeting with the bishops in Rome to share ideas, by writing letters to other bishops to help them teach the people, by creating groups and organizations to help all people, and by traveling to different countries.

Pope   Bishop   Priest   Parishioner

Commissioner   Owner   Coach   Player

To help us understand what the baptized do in the Church, let's take a look at organized baseball. In organized baseball, everyone uses his talents to benefit others. Players on a baseball team use their physical talents to help each other play a good game. Coaches help meet the physical and material needs of the players by giving them equipment to use and coaching on how to improve their skills. Team owners hire the coaches, pay them, make team rules, and provide a stadium to play in.

Several teams together form a league. A commissioner, or leader of a league, organizes the teams. He helps all players to know when it's time for their teams to play, to understand the rules of the game and to play fairly, to celebrate championships, and to use their talents to benefit all the teams.

The Church is something like organized baseball. Everyone uses his talents to benefit others. Within the Church, all of the baptized try to use their talents to benefit others by meeting their physical and material needs. Priests primarily help all people celebrate the sacraments and receive God's life. But priests, deacons, and volunteers also work together to form groups that prepare the church for Mass, assist during Mass, and donate food, clothing, shelter, time, talents, and money to care for the physical health, happiness, and well-being of others.

LIVING THE LESSON

1. How can we help everyone within our own families?

   _____

   _____

   _____

   _____

2. What do parishes do to help meet the physical and material needs of others?

   _____

   _____

   _____

   _____

3. How does the diocese meet the physical and material needs of others?

   _____

   _____

   _____

   _____

4. Who is a very special bishop, the leader of the universal Church, and the successor of Peter?

   _____

   _____

   _____

   _____

5. How does the universal Church help meet the physical and material needs of others?

_____

_____

_____

_____

6. How does the Pope know when there are problems that need his help in the parishes and dioceses around the world?

_____

_____

_____

_____

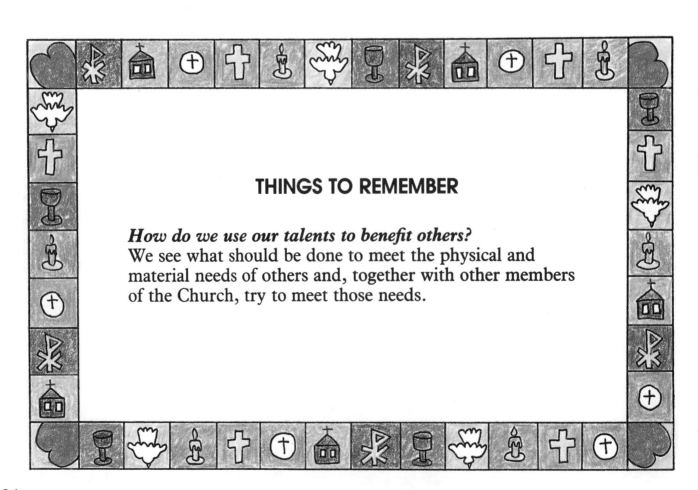

THINGS TO REMEMBER

How do we use our talents to benefit others?
We see what should be done to meet the physical and material needs of others and, together with other members of the Church, try to meet those needs.

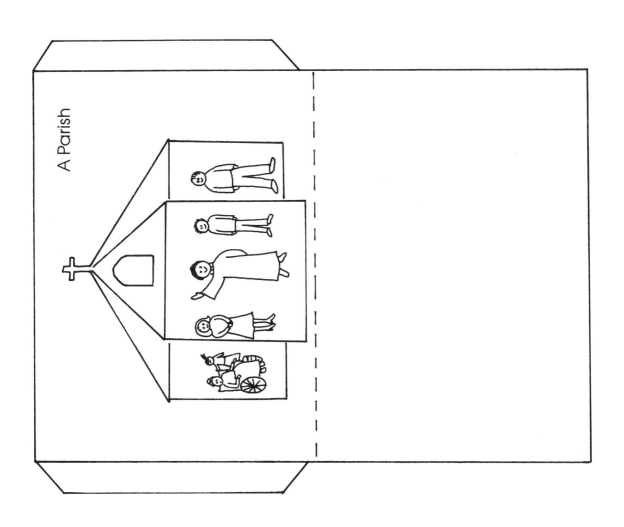

A Parish

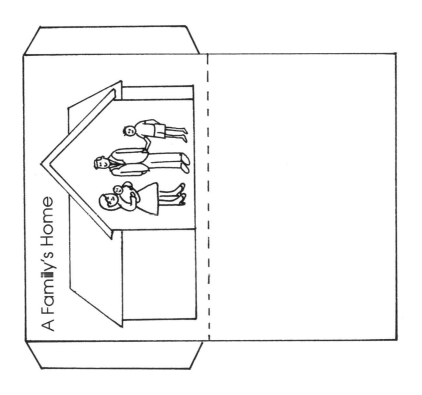

A Family's Home

195

A Cathedral (Diocese)

The Universal Church

20 The Gift of God's Life, Grace

Original sin damaged Adam and Eve's minds, wills, and bodies. After they sinned, their minds were darkened. From then on, it was not easy for them to know the truth. They did not even tell God the truth. Adam told God that it was Eve's fault that he sinned. Eve told God that it was the serpent's fault that she sinned. After they sinned, Adam and Eve still had the free will to choose to love each other as they should, but it was difficult for them to share that love because of original sin. It was difficult for them to act as images of God. They were tempted to think, say, and do things that they knew were wrong. Adam and Eve lost grace, God's life, because they sinned.

Although Adam and Eve did not return God's love, God did not stop loving Adam and Eve. He continued to love and care for them, but the love between Adam and Eve and God was weakened.

As descendants of Adam and Eve, we have inherited original sin and its effects. We are born without God's life. Original sin damaged our minds, wills, and bodies too. Jesus our Savior made up for original sin and all other sins. Jesus repaired our relationship with God and returned the Father's love. He helps us to return the Father's love.

Jesus' death on the cross was the greatest act of love ever. He loved from the heart. He did not love because someone told Him to do it. He made the choice to give Himself to God the Father and others through His death. He wanted to do the Father's will and give us a chance to share in God's life, grace.

If we are to love as God loves, we must share in God's life. Grace is God's life. Grace helps us to say "yes" to God. Grace enlightens our minds to know the truth. Grace strengthens our wills so we can choose to love. Grace helps us to govern our bodies. Grace helps us to use self-discipline in the things we do and say.

By dying on the cross, Jesus gave us a chance to receive grace. We do not have to die on a cross to show our love. We can choose to receive the sacraments and receive the grace that Jesus meant for us to have.

"A"

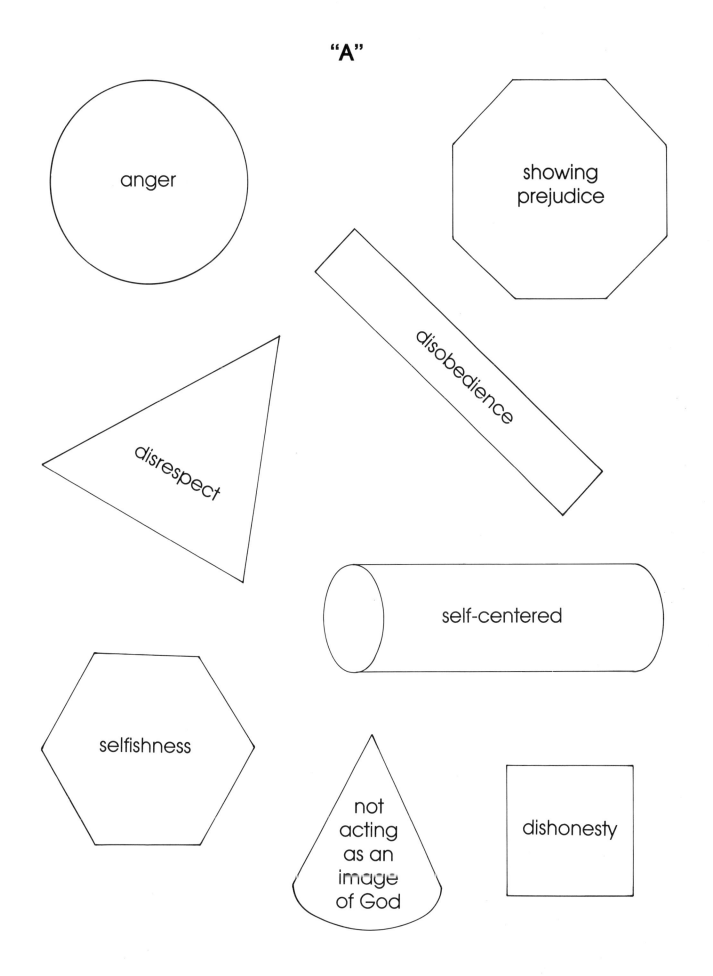

anger

showing prejudice

disobedience

disrespect

self-centered

selfishness

not acting as an image of God

dishonesty

203

"B"

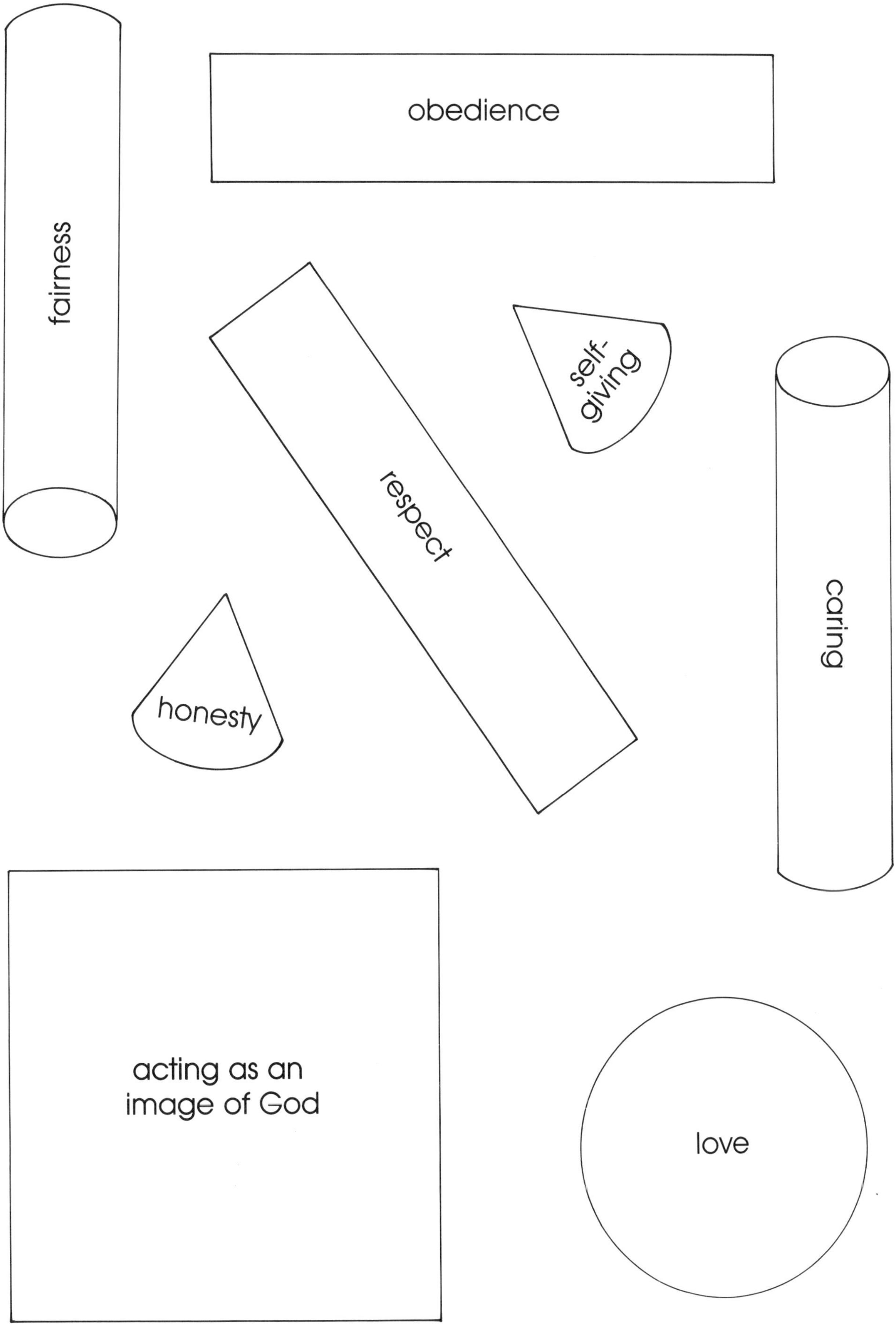

fairness

obedience

self-giving

respect

caring

honesty

acting as an
image of God

love

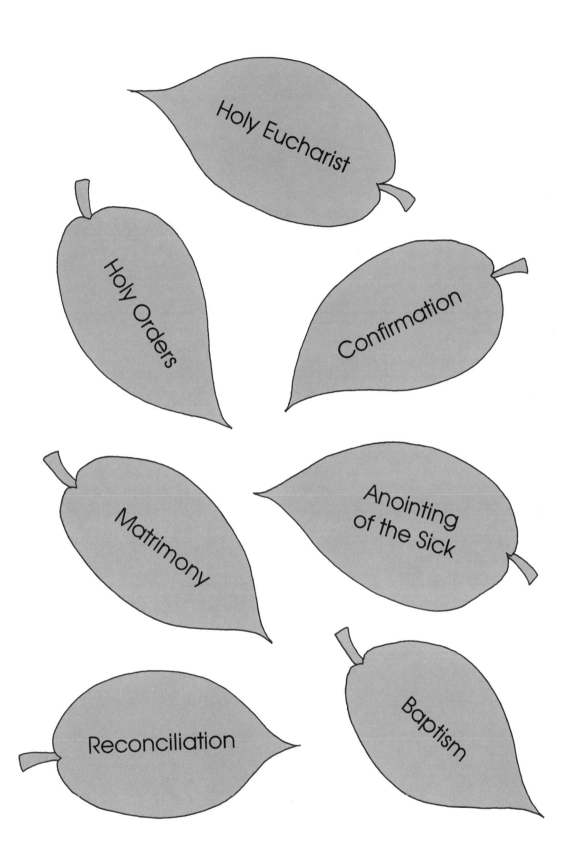

Before Jesus died on the cross, He knew what He was going to do. He knew that He was going to die on the cross to give us a chance to receive grace, God's life.

Jesus knew that without God's life, we would be easily tempted. Sometimes, we would not have the self-discipline to choose to do what is right for ourselves and others. We would say and do wrong things. We would be like the tree pictured on page 209. The tree is alive, but it isn't as alive as it should be, because it has no leaves. Without grace, we are still alive, but that is about all. We are not living as we should be, as images of God.

Because of Jesus' death on the cross, every human person is given the chance to receive grace. What a wonderful gift: the chance to receive God's life, to receive God's help in all that we think, do, and say, and to come closer to Him. Grace helps us to live as images of God.

There are seven special ways that we can receive grace. These seven special ways are called sacraments. A sacrament is a physical sign, given to us by Christ, in which we meet Christ and He gives us His grace. The seven sacraments are: Baptism, Confirmation, Holy Eucharist, Reconciliation, Matrimony, Holy Orders, and Anointing of the Sick.

Baptism

In the sacrament of Baptism, God gives us His life, grace, for the first time. Grace washes away original sin, makes us members of the Church, and makes it possible for us to live someday with God in heaven.

Confirmation

In the sacrament of Confirmation, the Holy Spirit comes to us and makes it possible for us to love God and others in a grown-up way. The Holy Spirit gives us the strength to be more and more like Jesus and think, say, and do the things we should.

Holy Eucharist

In the sacrament of the Holy Eucharist, Jesus feeds us with His Body and Blood. He makes us one with Him and with each other. We know that Jesus returned His Father's love by dying on the cross. Jesus' sacrifice of love on the cross is presented again for us in the Holy Eucharist. In this sacrament, Jesus stays with us in the tabernacles in our churches.

Reconciliation

In the sacrament of Reconciliation, our sins are forgiven. God's life becomes stronger in us. We are ready to do penance and to help others.

Matrimony

In the sacrament of Matrimony, a man and a woman promise to love and care for each other for the rest of their lives. They promise to act more and more like Jesus, in a loving and caring way.

Holy Orders

In the sacrament of Holy Orders, a man is ordained a deacon, priest, or bishop. He can then act for Christ in a special way.

Anointing of the Sick

In the sacrament of the Anointing of the Sick, through the anointing by the priest, Jesus gives comfort, strength, and peace to the sick, the elderly, and the dying.

When the tree has leaves, it is as alive as it can be. It is the same with us. With the grace we receive through the sacraments, we have the strength to live as we should, as images of God. We are as alive as we can be.

LIVING THE LESSON

Write the names of the sacraments underneath the descriptions that follow:

1. A man and a woman promise to love each other for the rest of their lives.

   _____

2. Jesus feeds us with His Body and Blood and makes us one with Him.

   _____

3. A man is ordained and acts for Jesus in a special way.

   _____

4. The priest blesses the sick, the elderly, and the dying, and Jesus gives comfort, strength, and peace.

   _____

5. God gives us His life for the first time and washes away original sin.

   _____

6. The Holy Spirit gives us the strength to be more and more like Jesus.

   _____

7. Our sins are forgiven. God's life within us becomes stronger.

   _____

There are other ways in which we can receive the gift of grace, too. We can receive grace through prayer, through sacrifices we make for others, through our helpful deeds, and through following the Ten Commandments.

When we pray, we turn our minds and hearts to God. We talk to Him, just as we would talk to a friend. But we should remember that God is more than a friend to us. He is our Creator, Savior, and Helper. When we talk to Him, we should always be respectful. We can show God how much we love and adore Him by praying special prayers that we know. We can also think of Him often during the day and talk to Him in our own way.

Write a short prayer to God, using your own words:

_____

_____

_____

_____

_____

_____

_____

When we make sacrifices, we are following Jesus. To "sacrifice" means going without something you like, or doing something that is hard for you to do, so that others are helped.

Jesus asks us to make some sacrifices. He showed us His sacrifice— His death on the cross. He shows us how to accept suffering and offer it to God the Father. By making sacrifices, we are strengthened by God's grace.

Doing a kind or helpful deed is a way of showing that we are images of God. There are many things that we can do to show that we are images of God. We can do things at home for our family. We can do kind deeds at school for our teachers and classmates. We can do kind deeds for ourselves. We all are capable of doing some kind deed each and every day. Each kind deed strengthens God's life in us.

Under each of the following headings, write three ways in which you can be kind or helpful.

HOME

1. _____

_____

2. _____

_____

3. _____

_____

FAMILY

1. _____

_____

2. _____

_____

3. _____

_____

SCHOOL

1. _____

_____

2. _____

_____

3. _____

_____

YOURSELF

1. _____

_____

2. _____

_____

3. _____

_____

OTHERS

A long time ago, God appeared to Moses. God gave him the Ten Commandments. The commandments tell us how God acts and how we should act as images of God. If we follow the commandments, we will be acting as images of God. Following the commandments strengthens God's life in us.

With a partner, look up the Ten Commandments and explain them in your own words.

1. _____

_____

2. _____

_____

3. _____

_____

4. _____

_____

5. _____

_____

6. _____

_____

7. _____

_____

8. _____

_____

9. _____

_____

10. _____

_____

Zacchaeus, a rich tax-collector who lived in the town of Jericho, was not a popular man. He always seemed to be collecting money from the people, and they wanted nothing to do with him.

One day, Jesus was passing through Jericho. Zacchaeus heard that Jesus had come to town. He wanted to meet Jesus very much—but so did everybody else.

The streets of the town were very crowded, and Zacchaeus was too short to see anything. He suddenly had a wonderful idea: he climbed a nearby tree and waited for Jesus to pass by.

When Jesus came near the tree that Zacchaeus had climbed, Jesus looked up and said to him, "Zacchaeus, come down quickly, for today I must stay at your house."

Zacchaeus was so happy, but all of the other townspeople complained. They said that Jesus was going to the house of a sinner.

But Zacchaeus promised to give half of what he owned to the poor and to pay back four times what he owed to the people he had cheated.

Jesus then said, "Today salvation has come to this house. The Son of Man has come to seek and to save what was lost."
—Adapted from Luke 19:1–10

Jesus went to the house of Zacchaeus to help save him. Jesus wanted Zacchaeus to have a chance to share in God's life, grace. We are all constantly being called to share in God's life, grace. We can answer that call by celebrating the sacraments frequently, by praying, by offering sacrifices, by doing kind and helpful deeds, and by following the Ten Commandments.

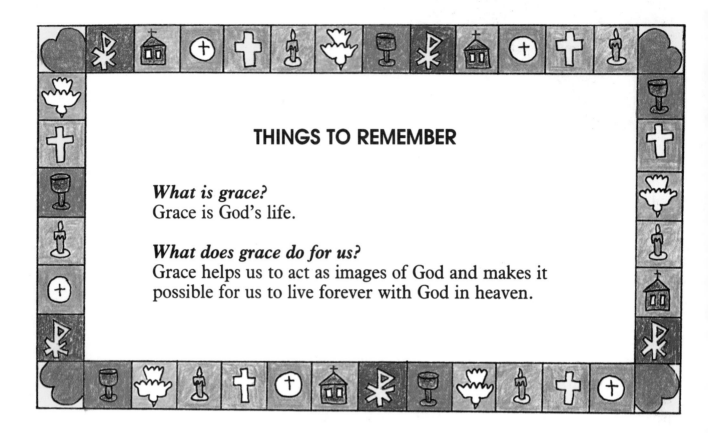

THINGS TO REMEMBER

What is grace?
Grace is God's life.

What does grace do for us?
Grace helps us to act as images of God and makes it
possible for us to live forever with God in heaven.

21 The Seven Ways the Church Celebrates: The Sacraments

WORDS TO KNOW

Sacraments of Initiation: The sacraments of Baptism, Confirmation, and Holy Eucharist, which make us full members of the Catholic Church, believing in Jesus and His teachings.

A sacrament is a physical sign, given to us by Jesus, through which Jesus meets us and gives us grace. Each sacrament is Jesus' special way of speaking to us, looking at us, touching us, and loving us in our lives today.

Each of the sacraments has a different physical sign. The physical sign is something we can see, touch, hear, taste, or smell. In each sacrament, Jesus touches us through the physical sign. His touch helps us. He forgives sins. He gives us Himself and helps us to love as He loves. When Jesus loves through the sacraments, He gives us grace. The grace we receive helps us to love Jesus and others. The sacraments put us in touch with Jesus' merciful love given to us on the cross.

There are seven special ways that Jesus speaks to us, looks at us, touches us, and loves us in our lives today. The seven sacraments are Baptism, Confirmation, Holy Eucharist, Reconciliation, Matrimony, Holy Orders, and Anointing of the Sick.

The sacraments can be divided into three different groups. The first group includes the three sacraments of Initiation. Baptism, Confirmation, and Holy Eucharist make up this group. Through these three sacraments we become full members of the Catholic Church, believing in Jesus and His teachings. We are called to love God and others as Jesus did. We are invited to worship in prayer and service. We celebrate Jesus' love.

In the second group are the sacrament of Reconciliation and the sacrament of the Anointing of the Sick. Both of these sacraments repair our relationship with God and draw us closer to Him. We can call these sacraments the sacraments of Healing. Through these two sacraments we ask God to bring us closer to Him and help us continue to believe and trust in Him.

The third group of sacraments includes Matrimony and Holy Orders. We can call these two sacraments the sacraments of Vocation. A vocation is a call from God to act as an image of God by loving others in a certain way. Through these two sacraments we answer God's call to the kind of life He asks us to follow.

We should remember that each time we receive one of the sacraments, God's life in us grows stronger. We grow closer to Jesus, and He makes us holier. The whole Church grows in holiness also and gives thanks to God.

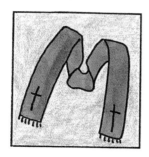   

BAPTISM

We all need Baptism because of the first sin of Adam and Eve. All people (except Mary and Jesus) are born with original sin, without God's life, grace. Because of original sin, everyone finds it hard to do what is right all the time. All people need God's life, grace, to help them love God here on earth by following the Ten Commandments, and to live with Him someday in heaven.

In Baptism, water is poured on the person to be baptized while the priest or deacon says the name of the one to be baptized and then says, "I baptize you in the name of the Father, and of the Son, and of the Holy Spirit." The water and these words make up the sign of Baptism. When we are baptized we receive grace.

In Baptism, Jesus touches us and helps us, because He takes away original sin. When we are baptized, we receive grace. The grace of Baptism helps us because we no longer have original sin. The grace of Baptism makes us God's children and members of His family, the Church. The grace of Baptism also makes it possible for us to love God and others on earth and to live with Him someday in heaven. The sacraments put us in touch with Jesus' merciful love given to us on the cross.

LIVING THE LESSON

1. We listen to and read the Word of God from the _____.

2. The place in which we hope to share eternal life with God is

   _____.

3. The person who usually baptizes is a _____.

4. The liquid used to baptize is _____.

5. _____ sin is washed away when we are baptized.

6. The men Jesus told to go and baptize all people were the

   _____.

7. At Baptism, the priest or deacon asks the parents what

   _____ they have chosen for their child.

B __ __ __ __

__ __ A __ __ __

P __ __ __ __ __ __

__ __ T __ __

__ __ I __ __ __ __

__ __ __ S __ __ __

__ __ M __

CONFIRMATION

Today Jesus continues to send the Holy Spirit. The Holy Spirit strengthens our faith and unites us more closely to the Church in the sacrament of Confirmation. The sacrament of Confirmation helps us love God, the Church, and others in a more grown-up way.

In the early Church, the Apostles celebrated the sacrament of Confirmation and gave the Holy Spirit to others. Before the Apostles died, they chose other men, called bishops, to continue their work. The sacrament of Confirmation is usually celebrated by a bishop.

The sign of Confirmation is the oil (chrism) and the words said by the bishop. The bishop lays his hands upon the head of the person receiving the sacrament. Then the bishop traces the shape of the cross on the person's forehead with an oil called chrism. As he does so, he says the name of the person and then the following words, "Be sealed with the Gift of the Holy Spirit." When he says these words, he means that the person is strengthened to witness to Jesus in a grown-up way. In Confirmation, the Holy Spirit gives people the grace to show by their words and actions that they are followers of Jesus.

When the bishop celebrates Confirmation, Jesus touches the person receiving the sacrament and gives the Holy Spirit to the person. He gives us Himself and helps us to love as He loves. When Jesus loves through the sacraments, He gives us grace, His life. The grace we receive in Confirmation helps us to love God and others in a more grown-up way. The sacraments puts us in touch with Jesus' merciful love given to us on the cross.

LIVING THE LESSON

You need not wait for the sacrament of Confirmation in order to be a witness to Jesus. All baptized people should show by their words and actions that they are followers of Jesus.

What are some ways in which you are a witness to Jesus?

1. _____
_____
_____

2. _____
_____
_____

3. _____
_____
_____

4. _____
_____
_____

5. _____
_____
_____

HOLY EUCHARIST

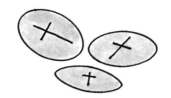

Just as we need natural food every day to keep our lives healthy and strong, we also need spiritual food to keep God's life in us healthy and strong. Jesus gave us the sacrament of the Holy Eucharist for our spiritual food. The Eucharist is much greater than natural food. When we receive the Holy Eucharist we receive the risen Jesus. He feeds us with Himself. We become one with Him. We are united with all His people who share the same food.

We usually receive the sacrament of the Holy Eucharist for the first time when we are about eight years old. We call this our first Holy Communion. After our first Communion, we should receive this sacrament often. In the sacrament of the Holy Eucharist, the sign is the bread and wine and the words spoken by the priest over the bread and wine. At Mass, during the Consecration, the priest says the words of Jesus, "This is my body" over the bread, and "This is the cup of my blood" over the wine. The bread then becomes the Body of Jesus, and the wine becomes the Blood of Jesus. Through the Consecration of the bread and wine, Jesus' sacrifice on the cross is presented again. Jesus' Body and Blood become our food and drink. At Mass, we can receive Jesus in Holy Communion. Jesus loves us so much that He remains with us in the Holy Eucharist after Mass is over. We can visit Jesus in church. The consecrated Hosts are kept in the tabernacle.

The sacrament of the Holy Eucharist is the greatest of all the sacraments. When we are nourished by Jesus' Body and Blood, we become like Him. He fills us with His love so that we can be more concerned about others. He gives us the grace to help us forgive those who hurt us. His grace helps us to accept sufferings and to make sacrifices.

In this sacrament Jesus touches us. His touch helps us because, in this sacrament, Jesus' sacrifice on the cross is made present for us. His Body and Blood become our food and drink. Further, Jesus remains with us in the tabernacle. He gives us Himself and helps us to love as He loves. He gives us grace, His life. The grace given in the sacrament of the Holy Eucharist helps us live our lives each day as images of God. The sacraments put us in touch with Jesus' merciful love given to us on the cross.

RECONCILIATION

Almost two thousand years ago, Jesus gave His life to save all people from sin. From the sufferings and death of Jesus we can see how terrible sin is.

The sins we commit hurt God, ourselves, and others. We commit a sin when we know something is wrong to do, and we choose to do it anyway. We know what is right, because God has given us the Ten Commandments. Sin can be committed by thoughts, words, and actions.

There are two types of sin: mortal sin and venial sin. Mortal sin hurts our relationship with God. When we commit a mortal sin, we turn completely away from God. God can help us feel sorry for a mortal sin, and it can be forgiven in the sacrament of Reconciliation. We cannot commit a mortal sin without knowing it. We commit a mortal sin when we do something seriously wrong, we know that it is seriously wrong, and we still go ahead and do it freely and willingly.

Venial sin hurts our relationship with God. It makes it harder for us to love God. It is still a sin, but it is not as serious as a mortal sin. Venial sin also can be forgiven in the sacrament of Reconciliation.

Jesus never sinned. As followers of Jesus we should try to avoid all sin. But if we should fail, Jesus will always forgive us. In the sacrament of Reconciliation, Jesus forgives all sins, mortal and venial, when we are truly sorry and promise to act as better images of God. We should try to receive this sacrament often.

The sign of the sacrament of Reconciliation is the sorrow we have when we say our sins to the priest and the words of forgiveness said by the priest. In this sacrament, Jesus touches us. His touch helps us. He forgives our sins. When Jesus loves through the sacraments, He gives us grace, His life. The grace we receive in the sacrament of Reconciliation helps us to love Jesus and others by helping us not to sin again. The sacraments put us in touch with Jesus' merciful love given to us on the cross.

MATRIMONY

Jesus loves us so much that He gave the Church the sacrament of Matrimony. In Matrimony, the bride and the groom say "yes" to marrying one another, "yes" to the promises they make to one another. The priest or deacon and two other people are witnesses to the promises the bride and groom make to each other and to God. The bride and groom promise to love and to care for each other for the rest of their lives—in good and bad times, in sickness and in health. Their love should remind people of the great love Jesus has for His Church.

When a man and a woman marry, they become a family. They try to make their love grow. Often their family grows to include children. Children are the greatest gift God gives to married couples. The child should be a reminder to the parents of their love for each other and God's love for both of them. Also, the parents' love for each other shows the child God's love.

In the sacrament of Matrimony, Jesus touches the bride and groom. His touch helps them because it makes it possible for them to love each other the way Jesus loves us. He gives them Himself and helps them to love as He loves. When Jesus loves through the sacraments, He gives us grace, His life. The grace received in the sacrament of Matrimony makes a man and a woman a family. The sacraments put us in touch with Jesus' merciful love given to us on the cross.

HOLY ORDERS

When Jesus lived on earth, He loved the people, taught them, and forgave their sins. At the Last Supper, Jesus celebrated the Holy Eucharist. We remember that Jesus asked His Apostles to carry on His work in a special way. Before the Apostles died, they ordained other men as deacons, priests, and bishops to carry on the work of Jesus. Today this ordination occurs through the sacrament of Holy Orders.

God calls some men to serve Him and to carry on the work of Jesus as deacons, priests, or bishops. After a man is prepared and approved by the Church, he is ordained. He is touched by Jesus in the sacrament of Holy Orders.

The man who is ordained as a deacon receives graces that make him able to celebrate some sacraments (baptisms and witnessing marriages) and to do works of love and charity. Through his works of love and charity, the deacon helps us to know how to love God and others.

The man who is ordained as a priest has already received the sacrament of Holy Orders once, when he became a deacon. When he is ordained as a priest, he receives the graces that make him able to celebrate all of the sacraments except the sacrament of Holy Orders. The ordained priest acts in the Person of Christ. He proclaims the Word of God and celebrates the Eucharist. He forgives sin and comforts the sick. He receives new members into the Church community. He belongs to the ordained priesthood.

The man who is ordained as a bishop has already received the sacrament of Holy Orders twice, when he became a deacon and when he became a priest. When he is ordained as a bishop, he receives the sacrament of Holy Orders again, in a special way. Through his ordination as a bishop, he is able to celebrate all of the sacraments and to teach as the Apostles taught.

The sacrament of Holy Orders is celebrated by a bishop. The bishop ordains men to carry on the work of Jesus in a specific way. The sign of the sacrament of Holy Orders is the bishop laying his hands upon the head of the man receiving the sacrament and the prayer the bishop says as he does this.

In this sacrament Jesus touches the ordained. His touch helps them because they can carry on His work in a special way. He gives them Himself and helps them to love as He loves. When Jesus loves through the sacraments, He gives us grace, His life. The grace received in Holy Orders helps the ordained man to love Jesus and all members of the Church. The sacraments put us in touch with Jesus' merciful love given to us on the cross.

ANOINTING of the SICK

Jesus loves all people. Through His healing touch, Jesus cured many people when He was on earth. Today people get sick, suffer, and die. Sickness and suffering are a mystery. If Jesus does not cure the sick people of today, He helps them accept their sickness or suffering in the way He accepted His Cross. Even the greatest sufferings can be tolerated when we compare them with the good that is waiting for us in heaven.

When people are very ill, or when elderly people are not in good health, the Church brings Christ's love and support to them in the sacrament of the Anointing of the Sick. Those who receive the sacrament ask for Jesus' comfort. This sacrament helps them to accept their sickness and suffering as Jesus accepted His Cross. It also gives sick people the strength to offer these sufferings to God.

The sacrament of the Anointing of the Sick may be celebrated in a person's home, in a church, in a hospital, or in a nursing home. It can be celebrated during Mass. People may be anointed more than once during their lives. The sign of the sacrament of the Anointing of the Sick is the prayer the priest says and the oil with which he anoints the forehead and hands of a person. In this sacrament, Jesus touches the person, forgives the person's sins, and draws the person closer to God. Sometimes Jesus restores sick and suffering people to health through the sacrament of the Anointing of the Sick.

In this sacrament Jesus touches us. His touch helps us to accept sickness or suffering the way He accepted His Cross. He gives us Himself and helps us to love as He loves. When Jesus loves through the sacraments, He gives us grace, His life. The grace we receive in the sacrament of the Anointing of the Sick helps us to offer our sufferings to God. The sacraments put us in touch with Jesus' merciful love given to us on the cross.

LIVING THE LESSON

Name That Sacrament

1. The sacrament that joins a man and a woman who promise to love and care for each other for their entire lives.

   The sacrament of _____ .

2. The sacrament that cleanses us from original sin, gives us a share in God's life of grace, and makes us members of the Church.

   The sacrament of _____ .

3. The sacrament in which Jesus forgives our sins. This sacrament brings us closer to God.

   The sacrament of _____ .

4. The sacrament by which the Holy Spirit helps us to love God, the Church, and others in a more grown-up way.

   The sacrament of _____ .

5. This is the greatest sacrament because it is the risen Jesus. He feeds us and unites us with Himself and one another.

   The sacrament of _____ .

6. The sacrament that helps people accept their sickness and suffering and offers Jesus' comfort.

   The sacrament of _____ .

7. The sacrament that makes a man an ordained deacon, priest, or bishop so that he can act for Jesus in a special way.

   The sacrament of _____ .

THINGS TO REMEMBER

What is a sacrament?
A physical sign, given to us by Jesus, through which Jesus meets us and gives us grace.

How many sacraments are there?
There are seven sacraments.

How does Jesus do His work in the world today?
Through the Church's teachings, sacraments, and other works of love.

Review the Ten Commandments

We learned in Unit 3 that God gave Moses the Ten Commandments on Mount Sinai. The Ten Commandments tell us how God acts and how we should act as images of God.

In the activity below, match the letter in front of the phrase to the rest of the sentence. On the blank line, write the letter of the matching phrase that you choose.

_____ The first three commandments tell us

a. *You will not have other gods besides Me.*

_____ I am the Lord, your God.

b. *to love and worship only Him.*

_____ In the first commandment, God is asking us

c. *of the Lord your God in vain.*

_____ You will not take the name

d. *about God and how we should love Him.*

_____ The second commandment tells us that we should not

e. *use God's name in a wrong way.*

_____ Remember to keep holy

f. *the Sabbath Day.*

____ The third commandment tells us

____ The last seven commandments tell us

____ Honor your

____ The fourth commandment asks

____ The fifth commandment says: You will not

____ We follow the fifth commandment by

____ You will not commit

____ The sixth commandment asks us to

____ The seventh commandment says: You will not

____ The seventh commandment asks us not to

____ You will not bear

____ The eighth commandment tells us that,

____ You will not covet

____ The ninth commandment asks us to

____ You will not covet anything that belongs

____ The tenth commandment tells us that we should

g. *loving parents to care for their children and loving children to obey their parents.*

h. *kill.*

i. *taking care of our own bodies and not hurting others.*

j. *how to love ourselves and others the way God loves us and others.*

k. *father and your mother.*

l. *to give Sundays and holy days to God.*

m. *your neighbor's wife.*

n. *adultery.*

o. *make promises we can keep and to respect the dignity of other person's bodies.*

p. *to your neighbor.*

q. *respect the freedom of others and not think of them as objects to be owned.*

r. *as images of God, we should tell the truth.*

s. *take something that belongs to someone else or damage the property of others.*

t. *steal.*

u. *be satisfied with what we own.*

v. *false witness against your neighbor.*

Unit 6
Liturgical Seasons and Holidays

ADVENT WAITING FOR JESUS

WORDS TO KNOW

Savior: Jesus Christ, the second Person of the Blessed Trinity, Who became man.

family tree: A list of family members in order of birth that, when finished, looks like a tree.

generation: A group of family members who are about the same age.

diagram: Drawing or chart that explains something.

covenant: A promise of love between God and people spoken in words and shown in acts.

sacrifice: An action by which someone or something is offered to God as a sign of love.

Pharaoh: The name given to ancient Egypt's rulers.

famine: A long-lasting and severe shortage of food.

anoint: To bless with oil.

incense: Dried tree-sap that gives off a sweet odor when burned.

swaddling clothes: Clothes that are wrapped tightly.

THE JESSE TREE

When Adam and Eve sinned, they lost the close friendship they had had with God. They also hurt their minds, wills, and bodies. God still loved them. But because they had said "no" to God's love and care, they could not live in the Garden of Eden.

Life was difficult out of the Garden. They had to find food and shelter for themselves and for their children.

Because He loved them so much, God promised Adam and Eve that He would send a Savior someday to return God's love and help them return God's love.

Thousands of years passed before the Savior, Jesus Christ, was born to the family of David.

The family of David was huge! After David, many generations passed before Jesus came. The Jesse Tree helps us understand when Jesus came and why He came. The Jesse Tree is a family tree. It includes the names of people from various generations of Jesus' family on earth. Most of these people lived a long time before Jesus did.

A Boy Named Jimmy Johnson

Every Christmas, all of Jimmy Johnson's relatives celebrate at his house. When everyone has finished eating dinner, Jimmy and his cousins get to do the dishes.

"Mom, we can't possibly be related to all of these people!" said Jimmy. "They must have come to our house because they knew I had to do the dishes."

"Jimmy," said Mom, "Everyone here is related to a Johnson in some way."

"Can you prove it?" asked Jimmy.

"Sure", said Mom. "Stop washing, come over to the table, and sit down. I'll show you."

"This diagram shows part of my family tree", said Mom. "This is my mom and this is my dad."

"Hey!" said Jimmy. "That's Grandma and Grandpa!"

"You are right!" said Mom. "Now, here I am, and here are my brothers and sisters."

"Some of us are married. These are our spouses. We form one generation because we are all close to the same age."

"You and my brothers' and sisters' children are from a different generation", said Mom.

"Can you name someone from your generation, Jimmy?" asked Mom.

"Sure," said Jimmy, "Ann Marie."

"That's right!" said Mom.

"Now count all of the people, Jimmy", said Mom.

"Wow! Thirty! No wonder we have so many dishes to do!" said Jimmy.

By looking at some of Jimmy's family, you can see how large families can get. The Jesse Tree shows us only a part of Jesus' family here on earth. The Jesse Tree gives you some idea of how long people waited for the Savior to come—many, many, many years!

Family Tree

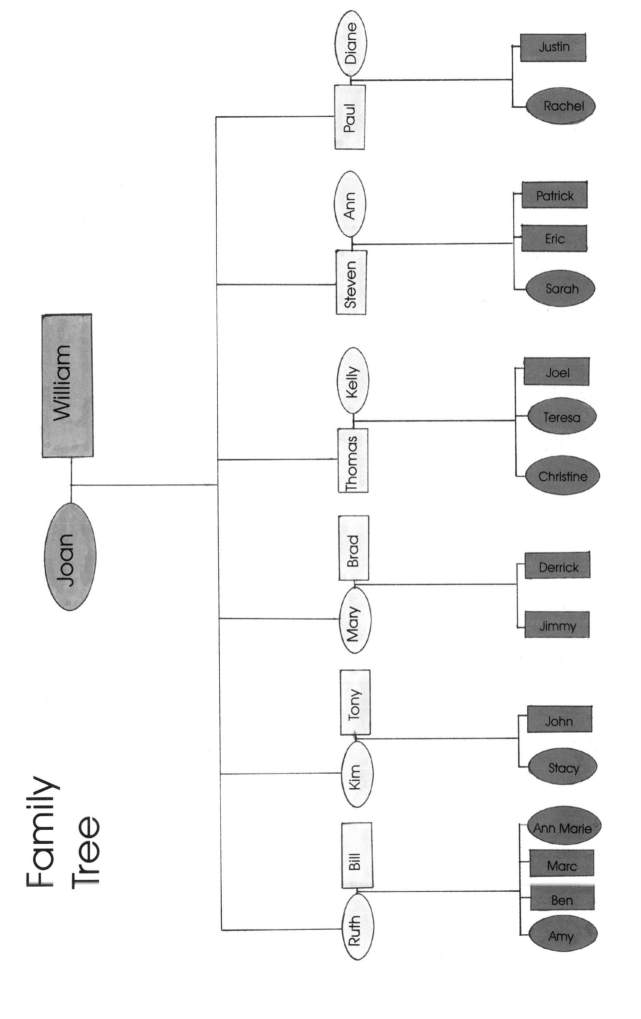

ADAM and EVE

When God created the world, He made all of the plants and the animals first. He liked them very much. But He also wanted to create someone in His own image, someone He could share His love with, someone He could care for. So He created two human persons: Adam and Eve.

Adam and Eve lived in the beautiful Garden of Eden. It had everything they needed: water for drinking and cleaning, and plants and trees with good food to eat.

God loved Adam and Eve very much. He wanted them to have everything they needed. He even gave them His life, grace.

God asked them to stay away from the tree of knowledge of good and evil. "If you eat the fruit from the tree of knowledge of good and evil," God said, "you will not be able to live with Me forever." In addition, by eating from the tree, Adam and Eve would lose grace.

Adam and Eve loved God. They obeyed Him, acted as His images, and stayed away from the tree of knowledge of good and evil until the devil came to visit them. The devil came disguised as a snake. The devil asked Eve, "Is it true you cannot eat any of the fruit in the Garden?"

"No", Eve answered. "We can eat the fruit from all of the trees except one. God said that we should not eat from the tree of knowledge of good and evil. If we eat from the tree of knowledge of good and evil, we cannot live forever with God."

"But that is not true", the devil lied. "God only told you that because He does not want you to be as wise and powerful as He is."

Eve knew the devil was lying. But she picked a piece of fruit from the tree of good and evil. First she tasted the fruit, then she took the fruit to Adam.

"Taste this fruit", she said. "It will make us as wise as God. It is from the tree of knowledge of good and evil."

After the first bite, they knew they had done something wrong. They felt ashamed. They heard God coming and they hid.

"Why are you hiding?" God asked.

"Because we heard you coming", they answered. God knew they had disobeyed Him and had eaten from the tree of knowledge of good and evil.

This sin of Adam and Eve was the first sin. It is called "original sin", which means first sin.

Adam and Eve had hurt the special relationship they had with God. They could not live with Him forever. They lost grace, God's life. They hurt their minds, wills, and bodies. They could no longer live in the Garden.

God still loved Adam and Eve. He made clothes for them to wear. He reminded them that they must find food and shelter on their own.

Adam and Eve were sad because they had disobeyed God. But God promised them that He would send a Savior someday. The Savior would show us who we are and how we should act. He would return God's love and help us return God's love.

—Adapted from Genesis 1:11–27, 2:8–9, 16–17; 3:1–23

NOAH AND THE ARK

 Many years passed. The earth was filled with people. Very few of them were acting as images of God. Noah, a kind and gentle man, was acting as an image of God.

One day God called down to Noah and said, "The earth is filled with people who are not acting as images of God. But you, Noah, are not like these people."

God said to Noah, "Soon a flood will cover the earth. Protect yourself and your family. Make an ark [a big boat] out of wood. Cover it inside and out with pitch [pitch is like tar]. Enter the ark and bring with you your wife, your sons, and your sons' wives. You will also bring with you two of every living creature. I will keep you safe in the ark."

Building the ark was not easy, but Noah obeyed God. Together Noah and his family worked very hard.

After Noah entered the ark with his family and two of all God's creatures, it rained for forty days. The flood came upon the earth. The ark floated on top of the water.

Finally, the rains stopped. The earth began to dry up. Then God spoke to Noah and his sons, "My covenant with you and all generations that follow you is this: Never again will there be a flood to destroy the whole earth and every living creature. This rainbow will be a sign of the covenant that I have made with you."

—Adapted from Genesis 6:8, 11, 14, 18; 7:1–9, 12–18; 8:6–14; 9:11–17

GOD'S COVENANT WITH ABRAHAM

After Noah, many years passed. A fine man by the name of Abram married a woman named Sarai. They were very happy.

The Lord then said to Abram, "Leave your country and your family for a new land that I will show you. I will watch over you and I will bless you. Your name will be great, and in you all the families of the earth will be blessed."

So Abram did as the Lord asked. He placed himself under God's care and took his wife Sarai and nephew Lot with him. They came to the land of Canaan.

Abram's nephew Lot was like a brother to him. Both he and Abram owned livestock together. Abram's herdsmen and Lot's herdsmen had a hard time keeping the livestock separated, so they had many fights. Abram did not like the fighting.

So he asked Lot to pick whatever land he wanted, and Abram would take the rest. Lot chose the valley near Sodom, and Abram settled in Canaan.

After Lot left, the Lord appeared to Abram and made this promise: "The land you can see will belong to you and your descendants forever. Your descendants will be great in number, and I will care for them."

246

After the Lord's promise, God changed Abram's name to Abraham, which means "father of many nations". Sarai's name was changed to Sarah, which means "princess".

—Adapted from Genesis 12:1–5; 13:5–17; 17:4–5, 15

THE SACRIFICE OF ABRAHAM

Abraham's wife Sarah thought that she could not have any children. Yet, when she was very old, she gave birth to a son. Abraham named him Isaac.

When Isaac was much older, God gave Abraham a chance to show his love for Him. He said, "Take now your only son whom you love and offer him as a sacrifice." Abraham was sad and worried. If Isaac were dead, he would not be able to inherit the land.

The next morning, Abraham, Isaac, and two of his servants split wood for the sacrifice and took it to the place God had told them.

On the way, Isaac asked Abraham, "My father! Here are the fire and the wood, but where is the lamb for the sacrifice?"

Abraham answered, "God will provide the lamb, my son."

When they came to the place for the sacrifice, Abraham built an altar.

As Abraham was about to offer the sacrifice, an angel of the Lord called him. "Abraham, Abraham! Do nothing to Isaac. For now I know that you love God."

Then Abraham noticed a ram caught in the bushes. "The Lord really did provide the lamb for the sacrifice!" he thought.

So Abraham offered up a ram instead of his son. God had cared for Abraham and Isaac.

—Adapted from Genesis 21:1–3; 22:1–3, 7–14

JACOB'S DREAM

Isaac's two sons were Esau and Jacob. Esau loved to hunt, which pleased his father very much. Jacob liked to stay at home.

One night Jacob had a dream. In his dream, a ladder that reached heaven was placed right next to where he was sleeping! Angels were climbing up and down the ladder. God stood above the ladder and said, "The land on which you are sleeping I will give to you and your descendants. I will care for you and your descendants, and in you, Jacob, all of the families of the earth will be blessed."

—Adapted from Genesis 25:21–27; 28:11–15

JOSEPH FORGIVES HIS BROTHERS

Jacob's youngest son, Joseph, was tending sheep in the fields with his elder brothers. His brothers were not taking care of the sheep. When Joseph got home, he told his father about them.

Jacob loved Joseph more than the others. He gave Joseph a long and beautiful coat.

Joseph's brothers were jealous of Joseph.

One day, when Joseph was walking down the road to meet his brothers, they saw him coming. They plotted to put him to death. "Let us kill him and throw him into a pit. Then we can say a wild beast did it!"

But one of the brothers, Reuben, told the others not to kill Joseph. Reuben told them to throw Joseph into a pit and leave him there. Reuben planned to come back secretly and rescue Joseph.

When Joseph reached his brothers, they stripped him of the beautiful coat his father had given him. Then they threw him into the empty pit.

But before Reuben could come back to get Joseph, the other brothers sold Joseph to traveling strangers who took him to Egypt. There Joseph became the slave of an Egyptian master.

Joseph was a very good slave. He knew that God was always with him, even when his master decided to put him in jail for something he did not do.

While he was in jail, Joseph used a special gift that God gave him. Joseph told people what their dreams meant. The Pharaoh heard about Joseph's gift and sent for him.

After the Pharaoh told Joseph about two of his dreams, Joseph said, "Both of your dreams mean the same thing. There will be seven years of good harvests and seven years of bad harvests. In the seven years of good harvests, save some of the food for the famine that is to come."

The Pharaoh thanked Joseph by putting him in charge of his palace and the land of Egypt. Joseph was good at his job. He saved enough food for the time of famine. He was kind to the people of Egypt. When his brothers came to Egypt for food, Joseph gave them some. He even forgave his brothers for what they had done to him.

Before he died, Joseph said to his brothers, "God will care for you. He will bring you to the land that He promised to Abraham, Isaac, and Jacob."

Joseph died of old age. He was buried in Egypt.

—Adapted from Genesis 37:2–4, 18–30; 39:1–6, 11–23;
40:1–23; 41:12–49, 56–57; 45:4–14; 50:24–26

MOSES LEADS THE ISRAELITES OUT OF EGYPT

 Joseph and his brothers grew up, got married, and had many children. When their children grew up, they had many children. The descendants of Joseph and his brothers are called Israelites. The Israelite community grew larger and larger.

The presence of so many Israelites in Egypt worried the Pharaoh. He did not want these Israelite children to grow up and take over his kingdom. He knew that he had to come up with a plan to make the Israelite families smaller. So he told his workers to take every Israelite baby boy away from his family.

During this time, a baby boy was born to an Israelite woman. The mother hid her baby so that the Pharaoh's men could not take him from her. After three months, when she could hide him no longer, she placed him in a basket by the river, hoping that someone would come along and find him.

The Pharaoh's daughter was taking a bath in the river when her servants saw the basket. They brought the basket to Pharaoh's daughter. She opened it, looked in, and found a baby boy, crying.

The Pharaoh's daughter kept the baby and chose a kind woman to care for him. The woman happened to be the baby's own mother!

Because the Pharaoh's men were still looking for Israelite baby boys, the woman could not tell anyone who she really was. She was afraid that something would happen to her baby.

When the baby grew older, the Pharaoh's daughter adopted him and called him Moses, which means "I drew him out of the water."

After Moses had grown up, he wanted to help the Israelite people who were being poorly treated by the Egyptians. But he didn't know what he could do.

The Pharaoh heard about Moses' wish and ordered that Moses be put to death. But Moses escaped to another country.

While Moses was in this country, God called out to him from a burning bush. When Moses recognized that God was speaking to him, he hid his face, because he was afraid.

God told Moses that He knew about the suffering Israelite people in Egypt. God asked Moses to be the one to lead the people out of Egypt to a better place. God also promised to stay with Moses and the Israelites throughout their journey.

Moses did what God asked him to do. He led the Israelite people out of the land of Egypt.

Three months after leaving Egypt, the Israelites arrived at the base of Mount Sinai. God asked Moses to come to the mountain top. Moses answered God by climbing up the mountain to meet God.

God gave Moses the Ten Commandments to tell the Israelite people how to act as images of God. These commandments were written on stone tablets and taken down the mountain by Moses to the Israelites below.

Throughout the journeys of Moses and the Israelites, the Lord stayed with them and cared for them. Moses died before reaching the land that God had promised to Abraham, Isaac, and Jacob.

—Adapted from Exodus 1:6–10, 15–22; 2:2–11, 15; 3:2–10;
12:31; 19:2–3; 20:2–17; 31:18; 32:15–16;
Numbers 10:11; Deuteronomy 32:48–52

 # DAVID AND GOLIATH

After the people had entered the promised land, a war broke out between the Israelites and their neighbors, the Philistines.

The last battle of the war was going to be between a huge Philistine soldier called Goliath and any Israelite soldier.

None of the Israelite soldiers wanted to fight in the battle. They were too scared.

No one volunteered to fight Goliath except a young shepherd named David. He brought his slingshot and stones and stood before the giant man.

The giant man laughed at David but told him to step forward. David ran quickly to the battle line and shot a stone from his slingshot. The stone hit Goliath in the middle of the forehead and killed him.

Saul had David live in the palace with his son, Jonathan. David and Jonathan became best friends.

Saul, however, began to worry. He thought that the people of Israel might want David to be king instead of him. So Saul planned to kill David.

Jonathan heard about the plan and warned David. David escaped not only this threat, but several others.

Yet when David had the chance to kill Saul, he did not do it. Saul had been anointed king; he was blessed by God. David did not want to go against God's blessing.

After Saul died, David became king. God made a special promise to David. He said, "I will make a house for you. When your days on earth are over, I will raise up one of your descendants. He will rule over a kingdom. I will be a father to him, and he will be a son to me. My loving kindness will always be with him."

—Adapted from 1 Samuel 17:1–11, 32–50;
18:1–11; 19:1–2; 24:5–14;
2 Samuel 7:12–15

THE BIRTH OF JESUS

Many generations after David, a man named Zechariah was offering incense in the temple. An angel of the Lord appeared to him. Zechariah was afraid, but the angel said to him, "Do not fear, Zechariah. The Lord has heard your prayers. Your wife Elizabeth is going to have a baby boy. You will name him John. He will be great in the Lord's sight. Many people will return to the Lord because of him."

In a city in Galilee called Nazareth, a man by the name of Joseph had a dream. In this dream, an angel appeared to him. The angel said, "Your wife, Mary, is going to have a baby boy. The Holy Spirit has made this possible. You will name your son Jesus, 'because He will save His people from their sins'."

Joseph's wife, Mary, also heard a message from an angel. The angel Gabriel came to Mary and said, "Hail, favored one! The Lord is with you."

Mary was afraid. But the angel said, "Do not be afraid, Mary, for you have found favor with God. You will have a son and name him Jesus."

The angel continued, "He will be called the Son of God. The Lord will give Him the throne of David."

Mary asked the angel, "How can this be?"

The angel answered her, "The Holy Spirit will come upon you." The angel also told Mary that even though her cousin Elizabeth was very old, Elizabeth was going to have a baby. The angel said that nothing is impossible for God.

Mary said, "Yes, I will do what the Lord has asked." A few days later, Mary went to the home of her cousin Elizabeth to share the news.

When Mary and Elizabeth greeted each other, Elizabeth was filled with the Holy Spirit. The baby moved inside her. Elizabeth knew what Mary was going to say before Mary told her. Elizabeth said, "Most blessed are you among women, and blessed is the fruit of your womb!"

Mary stayed with Elizabeth for three months. A short time later, Elizabeth's son was born. Elizabeth's husband, Zechariah, was unable to speak because he had not believed the angel Gabriel's message that in his old age he would be the father of a son. After his son was born, Zechariah asked for a tablet, and he wrote that his son should be called John. Then Zechariah could speak.

Zechariah was so happy. He praised and thanked God for his wonderful son.

Everyone in town was surprised that Zechariah could speak as soon as his son was named. They could tell that John was special in God's eyes. They didn't know that John would become John the Baptist when he grew up. He would help prepare the people for their Savior.

At this time, a census was taken to count the number of people in the country. Because Joseph's family was from the town of Bethlehem, he and Mary had to go there to be counted.

It took a long while to travel from Nazareth to Bethlehem. Joseph walked, while Mary probably rode on a donkey.

When they arrived, it was time for Mary's baby to be born. But there was no room at the inn. Joseph had to take Mary to a stable for shelter.

There, Mary gave birth to a baby boy. She wrapped Him in swaddling clothes and laid Him in a manger.

Some shepherds were in a field watching over their sheep. An angel of the Lord suddenly stood before them. They were so afraid.

But the angel said to them, "Do not be afraid; for behold, I proclaim to you good news of great joy that will be for all the people. For today in the city of David a savior has been born for you.

"And this will be a sign for you: you will find an infant wrapped in swaddling clothes and lying in a manger."

When the angel left them, the shepherds decided to look for the baby. It was late at night. The shepherds found Him in a stable nearby.

The baby was so wonderful! The shepherds knelt down in praise before Him. Before returning to their flocks, they told Mary and Joseph what the angel had told them. Mary kept these things in her heart.

The shepherds went back, praising God for what they had just seen and heard.

A long time after Adam and Eve had sinned, the Savior Whom God had promised was born!
—Adapted from Luke 1:5–20, 24–44, 56–66; 2:1–20;
Matthew 1:17–21

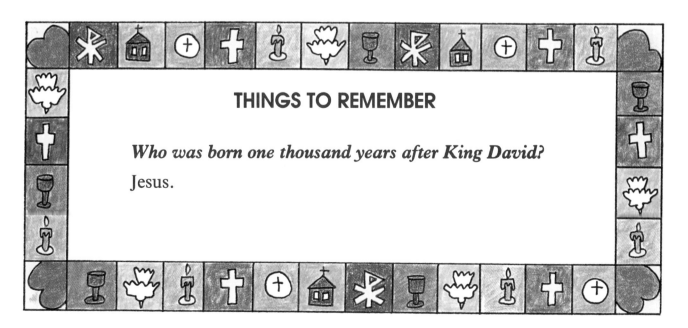

THINGS TO REMEMBER

Who was born one thousand years after King David?

Jesus.

LENT
A TIME OF PREPARATION

The season of Lent is a time of reflection and a time to prepare our hearts for the celebration of the Resurrection of Jesus.

In the past we may have forgotten who we are and made some wrong choices. We may have not loved as images of God should love. God's life in us may have been weakened.

Lent is the time to examine our relationship with God and with those around us. We need to take time to prepare ourselves to celebrate the Resurrection of Jesus and the new life of Easter. This new life is called grace. Grace is God's life. Grace helps us to act like Jesus and to follow His example. Grace also makes it possible for us to live in heaven with Jesus someday.

We start our journey on the road to Easter with Ash Wednesday. Ash Wednesday is the beginning of the Lenten season. The name Ash Wednesday comes from the ashes that are placed on our foreheads. The ashes are made by burning blessed palms left over from last year's Palm Sunday. The ashes are placed on our foreheads at the beginning of Lent to remind us of our humble beginnings and common end. We are reminded that nothing on earth lasts—animals, plants, and even people eventually die. But Jesus and His message are everlasting.

When the priest places the ashes on our foreheads, he tells us one of Jesus' messages: "Turn away from sin and be faithful to the gospel", or "Remember, man, you are dust and to dust you will return."

When we hear the priest say these words, we might be sad, because the words remind us that we are sinners. We like to hear good things. We do not like to be reminded of the wrong things we do, but these words can help us turn away from sin and love God more.

Now that we are older we can prepare ourselves to celebrate the Resurrection of Jesus on Easter Sunday. We have the Lenten season to examine our relationship with God and those around us. During each day of Lent, we should turn away from sin and be faithful to the Gospel. We should follow Jesus more closely and turn away from wrong choices.

If we properly prepare our hearts and minds during Lent, then Easter Sunday will truly be a time to celebrate. Christ rose from the dead on Easter, and we will rise to a new, strengthened life of grace. Grace will be strengthened within us if we have prayed, offered sacrifices, done things for others, and received the sacraments during Lent.

Someday our journey through life will end. All of us will die. But, by leading good lives as images of God, we hope to rise to a new and better life with God in heaven.

Lent is a time to prepare for new life: the Resurrection of Jesus to new life and the new strengthened life of grace, which we can have.

We can receive this new strengthened life of grace from God in four ways:

1. **Prayer**

2. **Sacrifices**

3. **Kind deeds**

4. **The celebration of the sacrament of Reconciliation**

When we pray, we lift our minds and hearts to God. We talk with Him, just as we would talk to a friend. Read the following story about two girls who are good friends and how they talk to one another.

GOOD FRIENDS

Amy and Mary are very good friends. When Amy talks to Mary, she usually greets her first. Then Amy shows Mary how much she cares about her and needs her by the words that she says.

Amy was at Mary's house last Saturday, and she enjoyed herself very much. Seeing Mary at school, Amy thanks Mary for the great time she had at her house. Amy senses that Mary is sad, and so, to help her feel better, she asks Mary to go shopping with her after school.

When the girls are shopping together, Mary becomes aware of how often Amy takes her places to help lift her spirits when she is feeling sad. Mary promises herself that she will try to do the same thing for Amy more often.

God is more than a friend to us. He is our Creator, Savior, and Helper. When we talk with Him, we should always be respectful. When we begin our conversation with God, we should greet Him by telling Him how wonderful He is. By telling God how great and good He is, we are adoring Him.

God loves us so much. We must remember to tell Him that we love Him, too.

Every day we are reminded of all of the marvelous things that God has given us: family, friends, talents, love, and a world to share. We should thank God for all of His gifts.

We can show how much we love and adore God by praying special prayers that we know. We can also think of Him often during the day and talk to Him in our own way. After adoring God and sharing our love and thanks, we can ask Him to help us, our families, and all people.

We should be reasonable in what we ask for. If we need the strength to prepare for a hard test, we should ask God for the strength to study, not for an easy "A". We know what we can do. We know what our talents are, and we know what our weaknesses are. Practice and hard work can sometimes change those weaknesses. We cannot expect God to change who we are, but He will help us become better images of Himself.

When you make a promise to a friend, you should keep that promise and do as you have said. Promises to God should be remembered and kept in the same way. For example, we should not want to hurt God with our sins. We should promise or <u>resolve</u> to try never to sin.

When we talk to a friend, greeting, caring, thanking, asking, and promising are usually part of our conversation. It is the same with God. When we pray to Him, adoring, loving, thanking, asking, and resolving make up our conversation. The Mass is the greatest of all prayers, because it includes all of these things.

Making Sacrifices

Prayer is one of the things that we can do during Lent to show our love for Jesus. Another thing we can do is sacrifice.

To sacrifice means to offer something to God as a sign of love. We make sacrifices when we give up something we like, or to do something good even though it might be difficult for us to do.

If your mom brings home your favorite treat from the store, and you eat only some of it and save some for later, that is a sacrifice. If you go outside and help your dad bag leaves instead of playing with a friend, that is a sacrifice.

When we make sacrifices we are following Jesus. By sacrificing Himself on the cross, Jesus shows us how to make sacrifices and offer them to God the Father. By following Jesus, grace is strengthened in us.

Doing Kind Deeds

Another thing we can do during Lent, and other times as well, is a kind deed. A kind deed is a way of showing that we are images of God. There are many kind deeds that we can do to show that we are images of God. We can do things at home for our family. We can do kind deeds at school for our teacher and classmates. We can do kind deeds for other people we meet. We can also do kind deeds for ourselves. We all are capable of doing some kind deed each and every day.

By doing kind deeds we act like Jesus, and grace is strengthened in us.

OUR JOURNEY TO GOOD FRIDAY

Directions: There is one stone for each of the days from Ash Wednesday to Good Friday. Write the date on each stone. When a day is completed, color a stone.

Happy Easter!

Prayer, sacrifice, and kind deeds are things we can do during Lent to prepare for the celebration of Easter. Another thing we can do is celebrate the sacrament of Reconciliation. When we celebrate the sacrament of Reconciliation we should be sorry for our sins and ask forgiveness. Read the story about the young man who was sorry for his sins and asked for forgiveness.

The Parable of the Lost Son

There once was a man who owned a great deal of land. He had servants who helped him take care of his property. He had two sons, whom he loved very much. The sons were given everything they needed to live comfortably—a nice home, clothes to wear, food to eat, and lots of love.

All the father asked of his two sons was their help in a small way with the daily chores. He wanted them to know how he ran the farm, so that when the time came for them to run the farm they would know what to do.

The older son helped his father. But the younger son became bored with the chores and thought he would rather have something more adventurous to do. He wanted to be on his own so that he could have fun and do as he pleased.

So the younger son went to his father and asked for his share of the money from the property. His father was disappointed that his son wanted to leave, but he gave him the money. A few days later, after the younger son had collected his belongings, he set off on a journey to a distant country, looking for fun and adventure.

Along the way the young man made many new friends. He spent his money entertaining his new friends. He found fun and adventure, but soon his money was all gone.

The young man's new friends all left him when his money was gone. Then a severe famine spread all through the country, and there was little food to be eaten. The young man was alone and hungry. He had no food, no shelter, no money, and no one to love him.

He finally found someone who would give him a job—feeding the pigs. The young man was so hungry that he wanted to eat the food that the pigs ate. All of a sudden he remembered his father and his home. How nice it had been to be well cared for. At home he had had everything that he needed. Here he had nothing. He longed to be back home again!

As he sat thinking about being back home he said, "Even my father's servants have food to eat, and I am here starving. I know what I will do. I will go back to my father and say to him, "Father, I have sinned against heaven and against you. I no longer deserve to be called your son." In other words, the young man was willing to work for his father as a servant. He started on his long journey home.

One day, as the father was taking his daily walk down the road, hoping to see his younger son, he saw a person walking toward him. He knew it was his son. The father ran to his son, threw his arms around him, and gave him a hug and kiss. The father was very happy to have his younger son home at last.

The young man, feeling welcomed home, said, "Father, I have sinned against heaven and against you; I no longer deserve to be called your son." He told his father he was sorry for his sins and asked for forgiveness.

The father was happy to see his son and forgave him. He called to the servants, "Bring out new clothes and put them on him. Put a ring on his finger and shoes on his feet. Find the fattened calf and kill it. We are having a feast to celebrate. My younger son, whom I thought was dead, is alive. He was lost, and now he is found. Let the celebration begin!"

During this time the older son had been doing work in one of the fields. As he came closer to the house, he heard a great noise. He asked one of the servants what was happening. The older son was angry when the servant explained that his father was giving a party because his younger brother had returned home. The older son did not go into the house to join the celebration, because he was so upset.

Soon the father came out of the house, touched his older son on the shoulder, and said to him, "Son, you are always here, and everything I own is yours. Let us all be happy, for your brother was lost and now is found." The celebration continued.

—Adapted from Luke 15:11–32

Jesus, like the father in the story, loves us, forgives us, and welcomes us back in celebration even when we have sinned. However, we should be sorry for our sins and ask for forgiveness.

Reconciliation means "to bring back together". Jesus knows that we are unhappy when we sin. We need a way to be forgiven so we can feel good again. He gives us one of His greatest gifts, the sacrament of Reconciliation.

We do not like to tell people when we do something wrong and are sorry, because we are scared of what will happen to us.

However, we do not need to be scared or nervous when we talk to the priest in the sacrament of Reconciliation. The priest is there to remind us that God loves us, and he acts in the Person of Jesus, forgiving us for the times we did not act as images of God.

In case you are feeling nervous, here is a quick review you can follow for receiving the sacrament of Reconciliation.

STEPS FOR RECEIVING THE
SACRAMENT OF RECONCILIATION

1. Make a good examination of conscience. Be ready to tell the priest your sins.

2. Go into the confessional and kneel down, or go into the reconciliation room and sit or kneel down. Greet the priest.

3. Make the Sign of the Cross and say, "Father, I have sinned. My last confession was . . . (tell the priest how long ago it was)."

4. Tell the priest your sins. When you are done, say, "I am sorry for all my sins."

5. The priest will talk with you and will help you find ways to be more loving to God and others.

6. The priest will give you a penance.

7. The priest will ask you to say an Act of Contrition.

8. The priest will give you absolution.

9. The priest will tell you to "Go in peace." Thank the priest and leave.

10. Do your penance right away.

We have to remember that the sacrament of Reconciliation is a great and powerful gift. We should take advantage of it frequently, not just during certain holiday seasons. Jesus wants to hear from us more than only a few times a year.

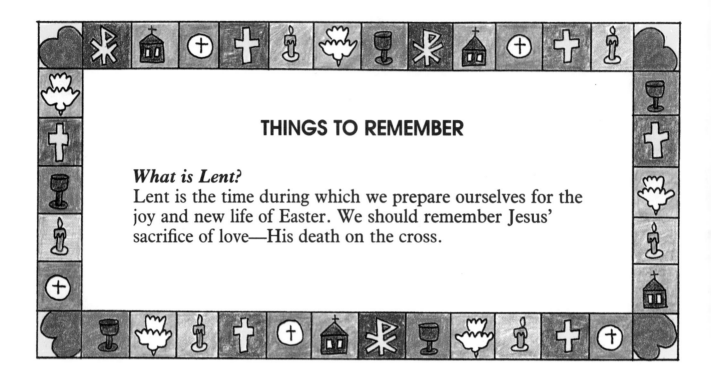

THINGS TO REMEMBER

What is Lent?
Lent is the time during which we prepare ourselves for the joy and new life of Easter. We should remember Jesus' sacrifice of love—His death on the cross.

The Saints

What is a saint?

The saints are holy men and women who live with God in heaven.
They followed Jesus' teaching and example while they were living
on earth. The saints loved God very much, and they tried to act as
images of God while they were living on earth. They had hearts
filled with love, courage, gentleness, and patience.

Some of these holy people became saints by doing very hard things.
They offered these things as sacrifices to God to show their love for
Him. Some of the saints gave up their lives rather than give up
their belief in God. Other people became saints by doing small
things very well. They offered these small things as sacrifices to
God to show their love for Him.

Who can be a saint?

God calls all persons to become saints. He does not exclude anyone.

How is a person named a saint?

So far, we have talked about how important it is to try to act as
images of God. If we do try, we are on our way to becoming saints.

Specific steps are followed when a person is named a saint. Here
are the steps:

1. A person is known to have lived a very holy life.

2. That person dies.

3. People pray to the holy person for help in their lives.

4. When their prayers are answered, the people report what
   happened to an official of the Church.

5. This official investigates the life of the person and makes a
   recommendation to the Pope as to whether or not the person
   should be declared a saint in heaven.

6. If the Pope decides that this person should be declared a saint in heaven, the Pope makes an announcement to the world at a special ceremony called a canonization.

7. In the Mass that is celebrated as part of the canonization ceremony, the Pope mentions the name of the saint in the Eucharistic Prayer.

Of course, there are many people in heaven. Some have been named saints. But others too have lived as images of God, have died, and are in heaven. Some of our relatives who have died are probably in heaven. These people are saints, too, but they have not been *declared* (named) saints by the Church. In heaven, then, we have the declared saints and also others who have not been declared. We celebrate all the undeclared saints on the Feast of All Saints, November 1.

ACTIVITY: Write about one person living today who you think will be named a saint someday. Remember to list reasons why you think this person will be a saint.

How can we become saints?

We do not have do great things to become saints. But acting like a saint can be difficult. We should try to act as images of God. We should try to do everyday things with love. We can look for times when we can do something or give up something for Jesus. We can do these things with love, and we can offer them as sacrifices to God. If we do these things, we are on our way to becoming saints. Being a saint takes a lot of love, courage, gentleness, and patience.

ACTIVITY: Make a list of three things you can do to become a more saintly person.

1. _____

_____

2. _____

_____

3. _____

_____

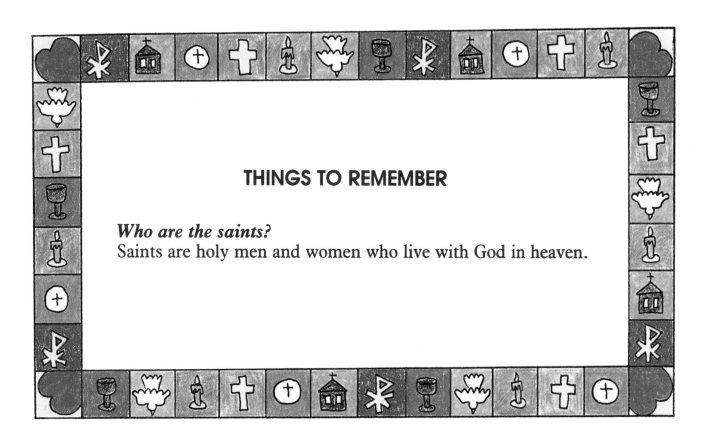

THINGS TO REMEMBER

Who are the saints?
Saints are holy men and women who live with God in heaven.